The Black Male Educator Guide to Thriving

The Black Male Educator Guide to Thriving

David Sandles

United Kingdom – North America – Japan
India – Malaysia – China

Emerald Publishing Limited
Emerald Publishing, Floor 5, Northspring, 21-23 Wellington Street, Leeds LS1 4DL

First edition 2025

Copyright ©2025 by Emerald Publishing Limited.
All rights of reproduction in any form reserved.

Cover image: Brickclay/iStock

Reprints and permissions service
Contact: www.copyright.com

No part of this book may be reproduced, stored in a retrieval system, transmitted in any form or by any means electronic, mechanical, photocopying, recording or otherwise without either the prior written permission of the publisher or a licence permitting restricted copying issued in the UK by The Copyright Licensing Agency and in the USA by The Copyright Clearance Center. Any opinions expressed in the chapters are those of the authors. Whilst Emerald makes every effort to ensure the quality and accuracy of its content, Emerald makes no representation implied or otherwise, as to the chapters' suitability and application and disclaims any warranties, express or implied, to their use.

British Library Cataloguing in Publication Data
A catalogue record for this book is available from the British Library

ISBN: 978-1-80592-474-6 (Print hardback)
ISBN: 978-1-80592-476-0 (Print paperback)
ISBN: 978-1-80592-473-9 (Ebook)
ISBN: 978-1-80592-475-3 (Epub)

Typeset by TNQ Tech
Cover design by TNQ Tech

CONTENTS

About the Author vii

Foreword ix

Acknowldgements xiii

Introduction xv

Real Talk xix

1. The Legend of John Henry 1

2. Thriving While Black: Inspiring Black Male Educators to Govern With Dignity and Purpose 15

3. To Sir, With Love: How Black Male Educators Foster Thriving Relationships 29

4. Thriving With Responsive Classroom Governance 47

5. The T'Chaka Effect: Black Male Educator Mentorship 61

6. Seize the Time to Thrive: Empowering Black Male Educators Against Racial Microaggressions 75

7. Thriving With Radical Classroom Instruction: Applying Black Panther Party Ideals to Foster Critical Thinking 91

Afterword 105

ABOUT THE AUTHOR

In addition to being a family man and a self-proclaimed comic book nerd, Dr Sandles is an Oakland native who served as a long-time K-12 teacher and is currently the Southern California Regional Director for CalStateTEACH, California State University, USA. Dr Sandles' interests include working out, reading, promoting Black male educator agency, and listening to old-school hip-hop and R&B music.

FOREWORD

Over a decade ago, I received one of the most jarring and frightening phone calls from my oldest son's high school. The Vice Principal informed me that the County Sheriffs were en route to arrest and take my son to a juvenile detention center due to a violation of one of their zero-tolerance policies: fighting on campus. Fortunately, when I arrived at the school, the officer opted not to arrest my son because the district policy was too excessive, even for the County Sheriff's office. Two years before our encounter with law enforcement, our son's school district encouraged interdistrict transfers from neighboring communities to enroll in their schools and benefit from its highly touted and reputable college-going culture. The district did not inform prospective transfer students that it was experiencing declining enrollment and that increased enrollment would benefit its yearly budget through average daily attendance. Simultaneously, the district school board approved a restrictive and punitive zero-tolerance policy designed to exercise control over the newly enrolled students, especially Black male learners transferring into its schools. Although my son was a Howard University scholarship recipient and recognized by the College Board as a National Merit Scholar, to the school district, he was just another Black male learner who needed to be governed by the strictest policies. Hence, he was continuously targeted and profiled by district administrators, teachers, and staff.

My wife and I frequently reflect on how schooling systems sought to deprive our two Black male sons of Black boy joy. Over time, we witnessed our loving sons become hardened by deficit-oriented educational practices that suppressed their voices and denied their existence. Their schools and district criminalized them before they were conscious of their black identities, compelling them to be more guarded each time they stepped foot on campus and grew older and self-aware. There were very few people at school, and in the district office, my sons could trust. It was a Black male Vice Principal who called the sheriffs to arrest my son. My wife, sons, and I worked relentlessly to survive despite the strenuous circumstances that beset us each academic year. Praise be to the Most High God; we successfully raised Black boys, but did not do it alone. It required collective action from our village to ensure their safety and well-being and to protect their spirits. Today, both sons are God-fearing, self-aware, critically conscious, HBCU-educated Black men—two beautiful and loving souls.

Unfortunately, there are far too many Black boys who are deprived of the opportunities to experience joy at K-12 institutions. Educational institutions are often assaultive and violent, undermining the endeavors of Black boys to become socially responsible and conscious Black men. I've witnessed institutions perpetuate a psychological attack against Black male students, as some of these learners enter school systems with the highest ambitions but exit believing they lack the intellectual capability to thrive in society. Many of these Black boys relinquished the aspirations that they once possessed as hopeful children because the schools hardened their hearts, compelling them to smile and laugh less. There was no sense or experience of joy in their classrooms.

I recently revisited my passion for classroom teaching at a Saturday School program, Sankofa Village. Recognizing its historical, racialized discriminatory practices, the district school board approved Sankofa Village, which was designed to mobilize and empower Black learners through a comprehensive, African-centered educational experience. The district requested me to teach mathematics to K-8 students and model for their teachers how Black joy can manifest itself in the classroom. My sons' disheartening K-12 learning experiences empowered me to transform my instructional practices. As a young teacher in the late 1990s, rigor was at the forefront of my mind. I wanted to ensure Black learners were prepared and disciplined to change the world. Today, I create lesson plans with joy central to the work. I integrate music into learning activities, provide opportunities for discourse on salient topics, encourage dance breaks as a mindfulness practice, and exemplify my joy through laughter and a sense of humor. Parents, students, administrators, and teachers have expressed that my class is different—students love to learn, enjoy the challenge, and, more importantly, relish the sense of community we co-created. One 4th grader shared, "You actually listen to us." I thanked him because his words helped me to realize that as I am making a difference, they are too. Their Black boy joy inspired and led to my Black man joy.

Dr David Sandles is a leader in this domain. His spirit is authentic—an aura that is endearing, warm, and encouraging. His pedagogy emanates from the Black Panther Party, whose members were astute and proficient in state statutes, regulations, and policy. They were creative and strategic in program design, recognizing the people's needs. Having known Dr Sandles for several years, we often talk about what is required to protect Black boys, and that inspiring them to reclaim and live with joy is imperative. As fathers, we share a common story and experience of what it means for

Black male educators to support Black boys navigating K-12 schools. We grew up in two different regions of California, northern and southern California, but we grew up in historically Black neighborhoods, Inglewood and Oakland, respectively. We experienced the brilliance of Black teachers, Black administrators, and other children who looked like us. Our churches were packed on Sunday, and the local clubs, universities, and sporting arenas had a vibrant Black presence. Consequently, we experienced Black boy joy, and as adults, we often laugh and experience Black man joy. It is our norm.

Sadly, many Black males are void of these experiences, and as I strive not to judge anyone's background, I often grapple with the thought that every Black boy should experience joy. Recently, I watched an Instagram reel of a parent secretly recording her Black male child doing his chores with a well-choreographed, yet impromptu, dance to Atomic Dog by George Clinton, during his 2025 Spring Break. With a broom in his hand, he moved like James Brown, Michael Jackson, and a member of Omega Psi Phi combined. The joy that emanated from the young man went viral, with over 140,000 viewers cherishing the moment with one comment stating, "I LOVE EVERYTHING ABOUT THIS!!!!" The young man's joy became our joy. It reminded me that we must normalize and ensure every Black male feels liberated to express themselves with exceeding and unspeakable joy in K-12 settings. We must restore, protect, and resurrect Black male joy.

    Dr Kirk Kirkwood, CalStateTEACH, California State University, USA

ACKNOWLEDGMENT

My family has always supported and inspired me, so I will detail their names and impact on me here. My now-deceased maternal grandmother, Georgia Ruth, remains the bedrock of my nuclear family. When I review my life, I am challenged to find important moments when she was not present and offered words of encouragement. Mind you, those words were always tempered with old-school Black admonishments, such as "...make sure you ask a lot of questions. A closed mouth don't get fed" and "You betta treat people right. You always catch more flies with honey than you do with vinegar." Adages like those are seared into my memory, and I am forever grateful to Grandmama for her life lessons and support.

My parents, David Sr. and Shirley, were incredible. They offered a firm hand in child rearing but balanced that with love, patience, and probity. As children, my siblings and I enjoyed family vacations, weekly allowances, and regular trips to the comic book store, where many of my foundational understandings were sourced. My parents are still family-centered and supportive, always supplying sagacious words and anecdotes.

Mike and Michele, my brother and sister, have always regarded me with circumspection. They had to always be wondering *Are we really related to him?* Despite my obsessive preoccupations with comic books, insects, and cartoons, my siblings protected me and continuously plied me with words of wisdom to keep me safe. "Watch out for..." and "If he ever bothers you, make sure to..." Without them and their reputations helping me navigate the social engagements of my youth, I have no doubt I would have been a street casualty, for East Oakland in the 1980s was no joke!

My wife, Carrie, has been my partner for so long that I cannot imagine a life without her. After our chance meeting at CSU Bakersfield on April 14, 1995, I had no way of knowing we would have a beautiful life together, but I am so content with the outcome of that meeting. As the late great *Prince* once crooned, *Until the end of time, I'll be there for you, you own my heart and mind, I truly adore you.* It ain't been easy by any stretch of the imagination, but I believe we were divinely inspired to work together on this journey, and

I am eternally grateful for the partnership. Because of that partnership, we brought our wonderful children into this world, each one a separate and amazing blessing. Daymon, David, Drake, and Daschl all have the best of our qualities, and it is beautiful to watch them blossom.

As of this writing, our family grieves the loss of our cherished Aunt Lois. Dr. Lois Webster Winston and Uncle Bill Winston epitomize how you do life. I am deeply indebted to Aunt Lois for being my personal cheerleader and for demonstrating how to serve as a leader. When I pass on to the next realm, I hope I was half as impactful as she was with those in my sphere of influence.

Coach Barnett was so much more than a track and field expert. Not only did I listen to him and *mostly* abide by his words, but I also often sought his guidance and actually enacted his suggestions. To this day, I regularly wear neckties because of the example set by Coach Barnett, an incredible representative of Black consciousness and professionalism.

There are so many others who deserve mention here, but I will respectfully call out the following as crucial to my development into manhood and during my transition to a professional: Coach Schwartz, Coach McSwain, Coach Johnson, Coach Jenney, Coach Owyang, Kempton Coman, Wayne Burris, and a host of other important men, women, personal friends and professional acquaintances. I would also like to acknowledge all the amazing men who are members of Freemasonry and Alpha Phi Alpha Fraternity, Incorporated.

INTRODUCTION

Black male educators seek to thrive. Black male educators want to enjoy positive student outcomes, they want to create powerful connections with the campus and community, and they want to be appreciated. Regrettably, those things are often absent in public school spaces, and Black male educators often find it challenging to endure. Consequently, many leave the profession disillusioned and dispirited resulting from the lack of connection and the absence of appreciation. As a Black man who served in public schools for nearly two decades, I feel compelled to speak to the challenges experienced by Black men teachers and the triumphs and opportunities to thrive that await Black male educators, some of the most vulnerable cogs in the educational landscape. I use the term *vulnerable* very intentionally, understanding that Black men are decidedly few compared to their non-Black counterparts, particularly white women, and because the experiences of Black males tend to be somewhat harrowing in K-12 classrooms. Here, vulnerability, however, also means that Black males who are serving their communities as teachers also leave the profession because of pronounced macro and microaggressions, resulting in part in gaping holes in the number of Black males among the teacher workforce. Yes, *vulnerable* has many dimensions, and it is often coded language that means Black male educators are an endangered species.

I also use the term *endangered species* with intentionality. While I am reticent to do so because of the pernicious, anti-Black historical associations with Black people and animals, the shortage of Black male teachers can be compared to the decline of endangered species in the animal kingdom, where the survival of a species is threatened by systemic factors such as habitat loss, environmental shifts, and exploitation. Similarly, Black male educators are disappearing due to deep-seated issues in teacher recruitment, retention, and support, compounded by a broader societal undervaluation of Black male presence and expertise in educational spaces. Just as endangered species face numerous challenges to their existence, Black male teachers struggle with biases in hiring, a lack of institutional support, and environments that often fail to affirm their cultural relevance. This creates a cycle in which fewer Black male teachers enter the profession, and those who do often leave at higher rates due to burnout or inadequate support, much like an endangered species unable to sustain itself in a shrinking habitat. The absence of these teachers weakens the diversity of the educational environment, denying students, especially Black and brown children, access to vital role models and perspectives while deepening racial disparities within the system.

To be clear, Black males are as varied socially, intellectually, sexually, spiritually, and economically as any people, so the overall discussion about Black males is only intended to generalize to the degree that Black males are a fledgling population in education spaces. Plus, much of the literature on Black male educators is suggestive of trends in the way they are perceived and treated. By no means does this book assert that Black male educators are homogenous.

Why This Book?

While this book is conspicuously intended to address the experiences and opportunities of Black male educators in the K-12 sector, some parallels may also be drawn with higher education, as those valuable educators endure untold challenges in securing tenure, being elected or appointed to various posts, and in being awarded research grant opportunities. Although there might be obvious parallels, separate tomes are needed to describe the challenges for Black males in that sector.

Further, while this work conspicuously offers scripted mentorship to male educators, it is patently clear to the author of this work that sexism and paternalism abound within society at large. Unfortunately, instances of discrimination against women are too numerous to name and have existed since time immemorial. Not only do I acknowledge those atrocities, but I also believe that through this and other works, people are actively seeking to disrupt those systems of oppression that continue to constrain and diminish our female counterparts. To be clear, this work is far from antithetically female; it is purposely seeking to lift Black male educators so students appreciate that powerful preceptors come in varying shapes and sizes.

Contextualizing the History of Black Males in Education

The 1896 adjudication of the *Plessy v. Ferguson* Supreme Court case provided a blueprint for separation and, inarguably, legalized inequity in the United States. For perspective, in 1892, a biracial man named Homer Plessy was arrested for traveling in a "Whites only" train. Plessy, who possessed comparably little Black ancestry, challenged the constitutionality of this law, citing a violation of the Equal Protection Clause of the Fourteenth Amendment. In 1896, the Supreme Court ruled against Plessy and upheld the notion that *separate but equal* practices could be applied in all quarters of society.

Relatedly, in 1954, the case of *Brown v Board of Education of Topeka* was decided. *Brown v Board*, as it will be called henceforth, overturned the *Plessy* decision and declared that separate but equal practices violated the Fourteenth Amendment, creating the theoretical possibility for Black students (all students) to have access to the same learning opportunities as their white counterparts. For many, this important ruling signaled a radical shift in race relations and the chance for educational and economic equality among all citizens. However, it is the intervening years between 1896 and 1954 that are of keen interest here.

In the years before *Brown v Board*, Black educators abounded, and unlike today, Black children could count the many Black educators who had taught them. After the *Brown v Board* decision, Black educators were routinely demoted, dismissed, or forced to resign from their posts, making way for waves of white educators. Estimates are that 38,000 Black educators were displaced from their roles serving students and connecting with communities in the twelve years after the *Brown v Board* decision. These forced changes had an injurious impact on education and the level of service in Black communities around the country. Further, according to Foster, there were approximately 70,000 Black teachers in the years before *Brown v Board*, about half the Black professionals in the United States. Speculatively, some contend that nearly half of those educators were Black men. What is certain is that Black males are presently sparsely situated across the educational landscape. In the decades since 1954, the number of Black male educators has steadily declined. At present, less than 2% of the national teacher workforce identifies as Black males, and the number is dangerously close to 1%.

With that background established, it is important to note that teaching remains a noble, rewarding, and challenging profession, and many Black males enter into the field to positively alter the trajectories of children in underserved communities. However, for Black males, teaching can become challenging for a whole host of reasons beyond planning, teaching, assessing, etc. With comparably few Black male educators in TK-12 public school spaces, the importance of nurturing, supporting, and developing Black male teachers is incontestably vital. Accordingly, this book features a set of guideposts for Black male educators to follow, and it provides educators with suggestions for thriving in this fantastic arena. Those ideas are represented in the magnificent seven chapters described below.

In Chapter 1, readers are provided a backdrop of the expanded roles Black male educators commonly undertake. Teacher, athletic coach, and resident disciplinarian, among other things, this chapter delves into the stress response to the expectations placed upon Black male educators. This chapter also provides skills for disengagement from John Henryism and healthful alternatives.

Exploring the imagery of Black male educators in popular media, student discipline, and suggestions for co-governing a classroom are examined in Chapter 2, and offerings are made for how Black male educators can effectuate positivity and honor in addressing student misdeeds (working with them to determine consequences).

In Chapter 3, Black male educators are encouraged to develop organic and meaningful relationships with students, peers, and administrators. Suggestions are supplied for how Black male educators can successfully navigate their interpersonal engagements and develop a relational agency that positively positions them to thrive.

In Chapter 4, the power of intentionally crafting classroom culture, student discipline, and co-governing the classroom with students is discussed. As Black male educators are often misunderstood and misjudged by others, it is crucial to have this brand of environment in place.

In Chapter 5, the power of mentorship is explicated. The need for Black male guidance in the educational sphere is immeasurable, so this chapter is devoted to making a case for every Black male educator to have a Black male mentor with experience in the field, and it challenges Black male educators to systematically commit to tapping into the mentoring resource, excavating the relationship for tips and tricks that are visible and invisible.

Chapter 6 examines the racial microaggressions and gendered racism that continuously vex Black male educators. Readers will also learn about recognizing these challenges and the techniques for overcoming them.

Chapter 7 provides insight into how Black male educators might develop the critical thinking agency of their students.

Each of the seven chapters enclosed also comes with anecdotes from Black male educators I surveyed. Over 2 years, I collected data from more than 125 Black male educators to learn their perspectives on a range of topics that ultimately became a template for this book. Each anecdote is in its original form and represents the thinking of the educator surveyed.

REAL TALK

For those who believe our society is post-racial, I must debunk that notion by informing you that society was constructed and maintained from an anti-Black viewpoint. Historically and contemporarily, Black people have been tolerated, contemptuously regarded, and continuously oppressed, repressed, and depressed most evidently since the year 1442. Within educational circles, there has been perfect symmetry with the larger society, meaning Black educators have endured racial indignities, toiled in poor facilities, and received desultory support in serving schools and communities. Even contemporarily, school suspension and expulsion rates for Black children are disproportionate to their population and outpace those of their non-Black counterparts. Unfortunately, Black educators exist within environments where this phenomenon occurs to their own people! As mentioned previously, there are also so few Black educators that a healthy sense of esprit de corps among Black educators cannot fully germinate. There are a host of other issues too numerous to list here, but, regretfully, many Americans intuitively understand those systemic features. Relatedly, according to researchers (Moss-Racusin & Johnson, 2016), male educators were perceived as more likely to be gay, viewed as a bigger safety concern, and found less likable than their female peers. These negative gender stereotypes are particularly pronounced among male teachers in the early grades (Bryan & Browder, 2013).

Given all the preceding information, many Black males weather their tenuous social existence and their often difficult K-12 schooling backgrounds to become educators, regularly citing their desire to appreciably change the school and community as the impetus for their work. According to noted researcher and author Marvin Lynn, Black men view teaching as a powerful opportunity to address and challenge social, political, and even economic injustices. In short, they want to make the world a better place. And, quite frankly, they often do. Black male educators are known for making profound, impactful impressions on students. Milner (2016) found that in one instance, a Black male educator reported on their effectiveness by constructing learning opportunities for his students based on what the students had taught him. That educator learned, adapted, and even incorporated Hip-Hop and other music genres to facilitate learning opportunities. Their presence in classrooms enhances the educational environment and inspires students who see their own experiences and identities reflected in their teachers. Black male educators also leverage their rich talents to address social and educational discrepancies and cultivate powerful learning opportunities for students. By building strong connections with their students, advocating for systemic change, and introducing diverse teaching methods, they are advancing their careers while also substantially altering the future of education.

The Adinkra symbol ⚫, used on the book's cover and throughout, signifies *strength* and *hardness*, for Black male educators have and continue to represent both those attributes. However, the symbol also denotes *perseverance*, a quality that any Black male who teaches must possess. The symbol also embodies a turtle and all its associated traits. Slow, methodical, and unrelenting, a turtle is often referenced in connection with the turtle and the hare fable, one that shows the turtle as a fighter and a champion for perseverance. As the story goes, the hare is endowed with incredible speed and agility, and the turtle is the antithesis. The two decide to race to determine who was better. Armed with hubris and incredible physical gifts, the race begins, and the hare takes the early lead. The turtle steadily plods along, consistently moving at the same pace. Meanwhile, the hare assumes such a seemingly insurmountable lead that it rests on the side of the road. The hare would speed past the turtle, gain a large lead, and rest beside the path. Before long, the turtle's steady pace won out, as the turtle crossed the finish line and the hare was in a state of painful disbelief, unsure how such an occurrence was possible.

The turtle in that fable is loosely analogous to Black male educators. Both push forward and represent endurance, power, and intellect in environments where others might be *perceived* as more talented, smarter, and more trustworthy. Despite those environmentally encoded microaggressions, Black male educators steadily progress toward greatness in connectivity with their students and community, mastery of their content, and development of their professional partnerships.

References

Bryan, N., & Browder, J. K. (2013). "Are you sure you know what you are doing?"—The lived experiences of an African American male kindergarten teacher. *Interdisciplinary Journal of Teaching and Learning, 3*(3), 142–158.

Milner, H. R. (2016). A Black male teacher's culturally responsive practices. *The Journal of Negro Education, 85*(4), 417–432.

Moss-Racusin, C. A., & Johnson, E. R. (2016). Backlash against male elementary educators. *Journal of Applied Social Psychology, 46*(7), 379–393.

CHAPTER 1

THE LEGEND OF JOHN HENRY

As children, many people were regaled with tall tales, nursery rhymes, and folklore that provide moral guidance, opportunities for language play, and a sense of why things exist as they do. Among the many tales readers may have heard is the one based on John Henry, a tale based on a Black man's physical prowess and exploits. According to legend, John Henry was incredibly strong and large from infancy, and his feats of strength as a child were awe-inspiring. So physically gifted was John Henry that in his role as a railroad worker, he was able to hammer steel into the ground with unmatched power and speed. His legend grew as stories of his ability to outwork machines, like the steam-powered hammer, spread throughout the communities. John Henry was said to be the fastest, most proficient at this job. Known as the *steel-driving man*, John Henry is often depicted with a sledgehammer in his hands and stands as a larger-than-life exemplar for others who endeavor to be great. However, there is a critical aspect of the story that is part of the moral or lesson, for at the end of the tale, John Henry dies, having physically overexerted himself in a race against a steam-powered drill many believed was faster than John Henry. In a hollow victory, John Henry won the contest but lost his life.

In some quarters, John Henry is praised as "the spirit of the working man" and "America's steel-driving folk hero." These monikers are symbolic of the perceptions rendered of John Henry and his resulting impact. In juxtaposition, Black males regularly assume duties well beyond their assigned roles to combat age-old stereotypes and ignorance of Black males. Erroneous and pernicious notions about the indolence and brainlessness of Black males pervade larger society and cause Black males to take on additional workloads to overcome those ideas. The assumption of extra duties, often more than any one person should bear, is described as John Henryism. Often labeled as a stress response, John Henryism is characterized as a "disorder, disposition, personality trait, or perfectionism" (McGee & Stovall, 2015, p. 498). In 1994, James coined the term John Henryism, describing it as the convergence of discrimination, overexertion in work, and the health challenges faced by Black Americans, particularly Black American men.

According to James (1994), John Henryism is a particular brand of coping that has adversely affected physical health in Black American adults by intensifying biological responses to stress. Research suggests that among Black American adults, this coping style may correlate with heightened depressive symptoms (Neighbors et al., 2007). It also emphasizes the poor health outcomes experienced by individuals who confront chronic stressors that exceed their ability to cope (McGee & Stovall, 2015, p. 498). This condition illustrates the significant spiritual, emotional, and psychological burdens placed on the bodies, minds, and spirits of Black men in school spaces.

As educators, it is common to assume duties such as lesson planning, governing the classroom, grading assignments, and delivering effective instruction to students. Among other responsibilities, these are hackneyed expectations. However, it is too often the case that Black male educators strive to outpace the negative societal constructions developed over the past few centuries by taking on added tasks and shouldering more work than their peers. These educators, aware of the historical and ongoing biases they face, often feel the weight of disproving stereotypes and combating the racial inequities embedded within the education system. Their roles extend beyond the classroom, acting as mentors, advocates, and sometimes even surrogate father figures for students who may not have role models who look like them. The added emotional labor that Black male educators often undertake, navigating microaggressions, addressing racial tensions, and striving to serve as visible symbols of success for their students, is frequently overlooked. It becomes a balancing act between fulfilling their professional obligations while also managing the expectations placed on them due to their race. This dual responsibility not only increases their workload but can also place significant emotional and physical strain on them, as they feel compelled to perform at a level that exceeds the norm, simply to be perceived as competent and worthy of their position. It is essential, then, for educational institutions to recognize and support the multifaceted roles that Black male educators play, ensuring they are equipped with the resources, respect, and recognition necessary to thrive in their careers without sacrificing their well-being. For perspective, A Black male educator shared with me the following tale:

> **Anecdote:** *Whenever there was something more to be done in the school, I was instantly nominated. Students misbehaving? Send them to Mr. Smith (fictitious name). Need someone to take students for an absent teacher? Send them to Mr. Smith. Need someone to plan for the annual Black History event? Ask Mr. Smith. There was never a shortage of roles for me to take on, and in my first year or two, I never felt I could refuse anything asked of me. It was tough.*

The Physical Toll of John Henryism

Regrettably, John Henryism brings about inordinate stress and compromised effectiveness, reinforcing the health discrepancies that Black men experience relative to their male counterparts. Health complications abound as a result of this stress response and many Black male educators labor under the crushing weight and cumulative effects of John Henryism. In general, health discrepancies between Black people and other groups lead to differing life expectancies. During the first year of COVID-19, the life expectancy of Americans dropped by 1 year. However, this was overshadowed by the drop in life expectancy for Black people, which declined by 2.7 years (Gilbert et al., 2022). While general life expectancies are also discrepant, this is in part due to structural racism and historical discrimination (Gilbert et al., 2022). Several challenges result from John Henryism, all of which are individually problematic, but spell disaster when taken all together. Issues such as hypertension, depression, and sleep disorders can plague Black males who are afflicted with John Henryism.

Often referred to as high blood pressure, hypertension, Hypertension, a leading cause of death and disability among Black people, is defined as having a systolic blood pressure of 130 mmHg or higher and a diastolic blood pressure of at least 80 mmHg. In the United States, this condition disproportionately affects racial minorities, particularly Black Americans, who tend to develop hypertension earlier than whites. Furthermore, control rates for hypertension are lower among Black Americans, with only 44.6% managing their condition effectively compared to 50.8% of whites. This contributes to serious cardiovascular health outcomes, such as heart attacks, strokes, and renal failure, increasing their overall risk of mortality from cardiovascular disease.

Further, undertaking incredible workloads in already toxic environments can result in depression in Black male educators. Studies investigating suicide specifically among Black men have found that protective factors include advanced age, southern residency, and robust social networks. Conversely, factors such as financial instability, job insecurity, living in areas of concentrated poverty, and physical health challenges are linked to higher risks of suicidal ideation and attempts. Notably, one study indicates that Black men with higher education levels may face increased risks for suicidal behaviors (Fernquist, 2004).

According to Adams and Thorpe (2023), suicide is now the third leading cause of death for Black males in the United States. There is ample evidence indicating that exposure to discrimination contributes to elevated rates of depressive symptoms. However, further studies are necessary to determine if a direct link exists between discrimination and suicidal ideation. This research builds on existing knowledge by examining how discrimination is associated with both depressive symptoms and suicidal thoughts among adult Black men.

The impact of discrimination on mental health cannot be underestimated, especially when considering the intersection of racial, gender, and socio-economic factors that shape the lives of Black men. Discrimination, whether overt or subtle, contributes to a chronic sense of devaluation and alienation that can severely affect one's mental well-being. Black men, who are often subjected to stereotyping, marginalization, and racial profiling, may internalize these societal messages, which can result in feelings of worthlessness and depression. These emotions, compounded by systemic inequities in education, healthcare, and employment, create a pervasive environment of stress that is not easily alleviated. Additionally, the stigma surrounding mental health, particularly in Black communities, often discourages individuals from seeking help, leading to an underreporting of mental health issues and, in some cases, an increase in risky coping mechanisms such as substance abuse or isolation.

Furthermore, the pressure to conform to traditional notions of masculinity, which often include the expectation to be emotionally stoic and resilient in the face of adversity, may exacerbate the mental health struggles of Black men. This cultural expectation discourages open discussions about mental health challenges, leaving many to suffer in silence. The resulting lack of social support and emotional expression can intensify feelings of hopelessness and isolation, further elevating the risk of suicidal thoughts.

Another reported effect of John Henryism is insomnia. Many Black men have reported that sleeplessness or the inability to sleep restfully is directly connected to the hyperactivity they undertake in the workplace. Predictably, adverse health circumstances can result when one considers the aforementioned professional hyperactivity and the lack of sleep often introduced into the equation. According to Smith et al. (2007), "When constantly confronted with racism, teachers can become hopeless, depressed, and begin to shut down emotionally" (p. 19). Smith et al. continue by saying, "This can lead to physiological effects such as problems eating and sleeping, hypertension, and other impacts" (p. 19). The cyclical nature of this issue is concerning, as the toll of consistent emotional and physical exhaustion compounds over time. Black male educators, in particular, are often tasked with balancing the emotional burden of challenging systemic racism while still fulfilling their professional responsibilities. This unrelenting cycle of stress, emotional depletion, and inadequate rest can contribute to a weakened immune system, increased vulnerability to chronic illnesses like hypertension, and a general decline in overall well-being. When sleep is compromised, cognitive function is affected, leading to decreased effectiveness in the classroom, difficulty making decisions, and even challenges in maintaining interpersonal relationships both professionally and personally.

Moreover, the stressors of John Henryism can be further exacerbated by the expectations placed on Black male educators to be strong, resilient role models for their students. This added pressure to uphold a *superhuman* image in the face of adversity can create an internal conflict, where the educator's emotional and physical needs are disregarded in favor of maintaining a façade of unshakable competence. The constant striving to outperform expectations can result in burnout and, ultimately, a crisis of mental and physical health. Therefore, addressing insomnia and other health impacts related to John Henryism is critical, not only for the well-being of Black male educators but also for their long-term effectiveness in fostering positive student outcomes. Creating a supportive environment that recognizes and mitigates the harmful effects of these stresses is essential for Black male teachers to thrive and continue their important work in the classroom.

More on Black Males and John Henryism

To be a Black male in K-12 educational spaces is to intuitively understand John Henryism. In general, the profession is laden with hundreds of daily decisions that would render many people useless. Tasked with detailed planning, managing student behavior, assessing student aptitude, and copious other responsibilities that are typical of teachers, Black male educators are also tacitly expected to manage not only their students but very often those of their colleagues, especially the boys. Even though the disciplinarian role is oftentimes antithetical to the dispositions of Black male educators, this can be the expectation, and negative labels are thrust upon Black males who refuse such undertakings. This added pressure can become a form of emotional labor, an unspoken burden that Black male educators bear, attempting to navigate and fulfill roles that may not align with their pedagogical approach or natural temperament. In many ways, Black male educators are compelled to embody a dual role: a teacher dedicated to academic success and a social enforcer tasked with reinforcing control in a system that often views them as the embodiment of authority. This mirrors the John Henry myth, where Black men, despite their strength and determination, are pushed beyond their limits, trying to prove their worth in a society that consistently undermines their existence and potential.

The John Henry metaphor is particularly resonant in this context because Black male educators often feel that to succeed in their roles, they must work harder, faster, and more efficiently than their peers. They are forced to outpace the systemic and societal barriers placed in front of them, all while being subjected to stereotypes that suggest they are less capable or qualified than their colleagues. This relentless drive can result in burnout, as these educators internalize the expectation to not only meet but exceed the demands of the job while simultaneously challenging the narrow confines of the roles imposed upon them. Despite their professionalism and expertise, they must prove themselves repeatedly in ways that are not expected of their colleagues, particularly those who do not share their race. In the pursuit of excellence, Black male educators often carry the weight of defying societal expectations and overcoming institutionalized discrimination, making their daily work an embodiment of John Henryism, a fight against exhaustion and systemic injustice that can feel both disempowering and ultimately unsustainable.

Anecdote: *When I was in my first few years of teaching, I used to go home feeling bone-tired. I'm talking about that deep fatigue, the kind you get when you are not just physically tired, but also emotionally spent. I was always trying to please my colleagues and give the impression I was a team player. I also found myself trying to fight racial stereotypes by always smiling and appearing happy. I was a clown. I would also volunteer for every opportunity, every committee available so that I would not appear lazy. The older Black teacher on campus tried to tell me, but I thought I knew better as a young teacher. She pulled me aside one day and gently told me that I needed to take care of myself. "Don't wear yourself thin trying to prove something to people who will never understand what you're up against," she said. At the time, I nodded, thinking she was just trying to protect me from being overworked, but I didn't really listen. I thought I could handle it. But over time, that fatigue started to become all-consuming. I noticed that I was becoming increasingly irritable, my focus slipping, and my relationships with both colleagues and students starting to suffer. Despite my best efforts to appear unbothered, I was carrying a heavy load, mentally, emotionally, and physically. The expectation to be constantly "on" and constantly performing, while also deflecting stereotypes, was wearing me down in ways I hadn't fully realized.*

Many Black male educators report that there is an expectation that they serve as the sports coach or the physical education guru on school campuses. This presents an inordinate challenge when one considers the typical teacher duties for which Black males are responsible, compounded by the additional responsibilities. Further, Black male educators must regularly participate in Black History or other cultural events in the course of their duties. While many Black educators voluntarily initiate and support such efforts, when added to the other tasks, the weight can compound and lead to frustration, burnout, and health maladies. Relatedly, because there are relatively few Black male educators, there is also the implicit task of serving as the expert on all things relating to Black culture. Apart from the Black tax this imposes, the practice of expecting a sole representative to have complete racial knowledge is wholly burdensome, unreasonable, and patently racist.

Learning to Thrive

Despite the foregoing information, the responsibility of serving as a teacher is an amazing and humbling experience that yields unimaginable rewards. Observing and guiding students' academic, social, and physical development is akin to the parent pride experienced when watching their child flourish. It is truly a noble enterprise. And, despite the potent impact of John Henryism, palpable techniques to overcome the psychological and physiological challenges are real, present, and accessible for Black male educators. Thriving is more than merely existing as an educator; it is enjoying, growing, and appreciating the experience. To do that, fundamentally, Black male educators should actively engage in the following suggestions.

Protect Your Time

One might ask *How does protected time work?* To thrive in school environments, Black males need to be protective of their time and energy, honoring their wellness while also equitably contributing to the overall success of school initiatives. This notion is antithetical to what our society has practiced and believed about Black men. Societally, we have constructed an image of Black men as beasts of burden, physical manifestations of toiling, who take on and endure more than their counterparts. Whether Black men are professional athletes or school teachers, the tacit expectation remains the same. To thrive in school spaces, to truly flourish, Black males must covet and fiercely protect one thing that has eluded Black men over the expanse of time since Africans were brought to the United States: they must intentionally control their energy, effort, and time. Since the beginning of American Slavery, there has been an almost maniacal fascination with the control over Black bodies and the maximization of productivity in terms of their time. Any perceived waste of time, however erroneous, and charges of laziness and cheating have been historically leveled against Black males. To thrive in educational spaces, Black males must identify their nonnegotiable time and honor it.

In and of itself, this is a challenge, protecting one's time suggests a selfishness that is atypical of community-minded educators (Remember, on the whole, Black men enter education for altruistic reasons). However, this is an essential skill that thriving Black male educators must possess. Quantitatively, educators spend approximately 40 contracted hours per week serving students and actively engaging within the school community. Beyond that, there are untold hours spent planning, grading, emailing parents/school personnel, etc., but for analysis, I will assign another 20–22 hours per week for that work. In addition, one has to factor in travel time to and from the school site (plus or minus 1 hour), sleep (plus or minus 40 hours), and healthy, mindful cooking and eating (plus or minus 5 hours). Most importantly, family time needs to be accounted for (plus or minus 15 hours). Given that there are 120 hours in a typical Monday-Friday work week, it is vitally important that Black male educators carve out time for themselves. Absent a desire by Black male educators to coach sports, lead campus efforts, or otherwise engage in extra activities, protected time is nonnegotiable to maintain one's psychological and physical wellness.

Black male educators should be judicious with their commitments to the point of selfishness. Added professional activities that detract from personal wellness and enrichment should be minimized or respectfully declined. Again, this can be difficult, particularly when the question of tenure or permanent employment status is at issue. For perspective, in many educational contexts, educators are probationary employees in their first 2 years in a school or district. During that time, school administrators scrutinize their performance to ensure teachers can effectively teach students, engage in professional development, and work well with colleagues, among other things. After the initial 2 years, educators are considered permanent employees. I would contend that Black males should artfully navigate their first 2 years to secure permanent employment. With this suggestion, I mean that Black males should invest in the school community in ways that promote school health while simultaneously deriving pleasure or building personal efficacy from that activity. The investment should be mutually beneficial. For example, if Black male educators are inclined to coach an after-school debate team and there is an opportunity to develop one's skills, leadership abilities, or professional networking opportunities, this role is symbiotic, purposeful, and will demonstrate value added to the school community. Beyond those first 2 years, however, I recommend that Black men become passionate defenders of their protected time.

To assist with the protection of time, please note the following techniques to be used in response to seemingly innocuous requests to take on additional duties:

1. Thank you for considering me for this additional responsibility. I appreciate the opportunity, but I want to ensure I can maintain my focus on my current teaching duties and effectively support my students.
2. I'm open to joining the school improvement committee, and thank you for considering me, but I'd like to confirm that it won't interfere with my teaching schedule or contractual obligations. Can we outline the time expectations?
3. My priority is always the well-being of my students. I'd like to discuss how these additional responsibilities might affect my ability to deliver quality instruction and support.
4. I would be interested in coaching the soccer team, but I would need to limit my commitments to one season to ensure I can remain focused on supporting my students.
5. I would be open to taking on this additional duty if it can be structured in a way that doesn't compromise my current teaching effectiveness and personal commitments. Can we explore how this might be achieved?

By using the suggestions above, Black male educators can demonstrate a willingness to actively participate in school-related activities while also remaining steadfast in their wellness. It was said somewhere that *if teachers only worked their contracted hours, 90% of what needed to be done would go undone.* If there is even a grain of truth to that statement, adding other responsibilities only further taxes educators and increases the possibility of burnout. The offerings above are especially useful during the teaching probationary period, the length of which depends on the state. During that time, neophyte teachers must understand that termination can happen for virtually *any* reason. Often, terminology such as the following appears: *probationary teachers may be given notice of nonrenewal effective at the end of the school year at any time without any statement of reasons or hearing.*

Once a teacher earns permanent status, I would suggest a staunch commitment to completing tasks *only* during contracted hours. Again, this may come across as selfish to some, but to those who are culturally and historically competent, this protection of time for Black male educators should be easily understood. Even for those lacking in cultural and historical competence, respect for personal time and family commitments should be easily understood.

Proactive Self-Care

Nearly every organization will tout the importance of prioritizing self-care among its employees, but the moment one attempts to enact a self-care plan, problems often arise. This is partly because there is not enough understanding of what self-care entails. Here, self-care is defined as proactively nurturing one's physical, psychological, and spiritual health. For Black male educators, self-care is important because, as noted earlier, the physical toll John Henryism exacts can be crushing. The weight of daily demands for student success, the appearance of having it all together, and the collegiality one is expected to possess are enough, but the additional roles for Black male educators compound the challenges and create unrealistic but typical circumstances in which many Black male teachers exist. An uncommon brand of self-care is needed to combat the potent impacts of John Henryism and ensure that Black males thrive in educational spaces and it must go beyond a bubble bath or a weekend off; it requires a more deliberate, sustained approach to managing the emotional, physical, and mental exhaustion that can result from constant overperformance and the demands of institutionalized racism. This might include creating intentional boundaries, such as limiting the number of extracurricular activities taken on or setting clear professional limits with colleagues and administrators.

Given the often overwhelming expectation to take on additional responsibilities, particularly around discipline and student advocacy, Black male teachers need to actively resist the temptation to overextend themselves, knowing that their well-being depends on prioritizing their own needs. A critical element of this self-care includes acknowledging the importance of community and seeking out spaces where they can speak openly about their challenges without judgment.

Another essential aspect of self-care for Black male educators is engaging in practices that affirm their identity and allow them to reconnect with the cultural and spiritual sources of strength that have historically sustained Black communities. This might involve engaging in spiritual practices, such as prayer, meditation, or participation in faith-based communities. It may also include culturally enriching experiences, attending events that celebrate Black culture or spending time with family and friends who share similar experiences. These activities help to replenish the mental and emotional reserves that are depleted during the demands of the school year. Moreover, when Black male educators take time to invest in their sense of self outside of the classroom, they are better able to approach their students with the empathy, understanding, and energy needed to support their growth.

Ultimately, proactive self-care for Black male educators is not simply about "resting" from work; it is about recognizing and addressing the cumulative toll of racial and professional expectations. It requires resilience, discipline, and a commitment to preserving one's well-being even when external pressures may suggest otherwise. Schools, districts, and communities must also take responsibility in supporting these educators by providing spaces for collaboration, mentorship, and emotional support. Only when Black male educators are given the tools and space to care for themselves can they continue to inspire and uplift the students they serve, particularly those who look to them as role models. By making self-care a priority, Black male educators can more effectively navigate the complex landscape of education, not just surviving, but thriving in the face of adversity.

Physical Activity

Participating in activities that promote physical health, whether it's through sports, dance, or outdoor activities, can be both invigorating and a source of joy. Again, although commonsensical, many do not partake in physical activity, let alone enjoyable physical activity. I am a proponent of walking, while one of my former colleagues advocates dancing, especially hip-hop or Salsa dancing. With the exertion required for any structured dance class, participants can likely lose weight, tone muscles, release aggression, and learn a new skill, bearing in mind that learning is an ongoing process. Many others swear by martial arts as a way of releasing pent-up aggression while learning something new. In addition, regular physical activity is known to diminish stress and anxiety, which is especially helpful for educators dealing with the challenges of teaching. When Black male educators incorporate exercise into their daily routines, they can manage stress more effectively, leading to better mental health. A positive mindset not only enhances their well-being but also translates into more effective teaching, as they infuse the classroom with their vibrant energy.

Minimally, walking a short distance each day will assist in creating a mental and physical release from stressors. Like many people who do not regularly exercise, the time constraint serves as a prime reason why regular exercise does not occur. To eliminate this possibility and to create a low-anxiety method for getting exercise, I urge Black male educators to walk around their block at least once before getting into their car in the morning and/or at night. Sometimes the idea of gathering gym clothes, readying to deal with other people (remember, educators already have to be "on" for many hours per day), and eating a pre-workout meal are barriers that will ultimately encourage inertia rather than engagement. So, a simple solution is to walk around the block, backyard, or on the treadmill for 10 minutes. Given the health benefits, ten minutes per day can go a long way toward helping combat some of the stressors many Black male educators face.

Massage Therapy

Within the challenging landscape of education, Black male educators often encounter unique obstacles that can lead to heightened stress and burnout. Integrating massage therapy into their wellness practices can provide a variety of benefits that sustain their physical and mental health while enhancing their effectiveness as teachers. Ultimately, this strategy can enable Black male educators to thrive through stress relief, improved overall health, and increased mental clarity.

Massage therapy is particularly adept at relieving stress and promoting relaxation. Educators regularly face considerable pressure to meet academic benchmarks and address the diverse needs of their students. For Black male educators, the responsibility is even greater, as they often find themselves supporting other teachers with discipline issues and navigating the gendered racism that can arise in their roles. Regular massage therapy sessions can alleviate muscle tension, reduce cortisol levels, and instill a sense of peace, allowing educators to recharge and manage their responsibilities more effectively.

Furthermore, massage therapy is essential for improving physical health, especially for Black male educators who may face higher risks of health concerns like hypertension and chronic pain. The stress that accumulates after a tough week can be significant. For Black males in education, the burden can feel exceptionally heavy, making massage therapy a valuable tool for relieving some of this tension and relaxing the muscles. Additionally, therapeutic massage enhances circulation, increases flexibility, and lessens muscle soreness, contributing to overall well-being. I suggest seeking treatment at least twice a month, ideally weekly if possible. I also encourage Black male educators to explore whether their health insurance covers some treatment costs, which could provide valuable financial support.

Conclusion

While the tale of John Henry offers a sobering account of the limits of human strength and the unstoppable force of technological innovation, it simultaneously supplies a window into the incredible weight Black male educators hoist regularly. John Henry's victory over the steam drill may symbolize the power of human will, but his death underscores the futility of competing with the machines that are transforming the world. Similarly, the educational community must grapple with teacher preparation features and in-service learning opportunities to support Black male educators meaningfully. Ultimately, John Henry's legacy endures not only as a monument to human resilience but also as a cautionary tale about the risks of pushing too hard against forces that cannot be controlled. Attention to protected time for Black male educators, proactive self-care, and other innovations in mitigating health risks should be explored and implemented. For Black male educators, the job is to thrive. The joys of teaching can be evinced when one has adequately attended to themselves and then the needs of the students and the school community. In this way, Black male educators can relieve themselves of some of the stressors that accompany their role, overcome the menace of John Henryism, and grow in the role of lifelong learners.

To Thrive, Black male educators should:

1. Protect Their Time
2. Practice Proactive Self-Care
3. Engage in Physical Activity
4. Seek Massage Therapy

Questions for Reflection

1. The chapter describes the emotional and physical toll of John Henryism. How do you think historical and societal pressures on Black males contribute to the extra burdens they carry in educational settings, and what steps can schools take to alleviate these pressures?
2. Considering the challenges highlighted in the chapter, how can Black male educators build a support system within their school environment to combat isolation and burnout? What role can collaboration with colleagues and students play in reducing the impact of John Henryism?
3. What practices can schools adopt to support Black male educators maintain their health and well-being, and how can these practices be integrated into their daily routines to prevent burnout, as highlighted in the chapter?

References

Adams, L. B. & Thorpe, R. J. (2023). Achieving mental health equity in Black male suicide prevention. *Frontiers in Public Health, 11,* 1113222.

Fernquist, R. M. (2004). Does single motherhood protect against Black female suicide? *Archives of Suicide Research, 8*(2), 163–171.

Gilbert, K. L., Ransome, Y., Dean, L. T., DeCaille, J., & Kawachi, I. (2022). Social capital, Black social mobility, and health disparities. *Annual Review of Public Health, 43*(1), 173–191.

James, S. A. (1994). John Henryism and the health of African-Americans. *Culture, Medicine and Psychiatry, 18,* 163–182.

McGee, E. O., & Stovall, D. (2015). Reimagining critical race theory in education: Mental health, healing, and the pathway to liberatory praxis. *Educational Theory, 65*(5), 491–511. https://doi.org/10.1111/edth.12129

Neighbors, H. W., Njai, R., & Jackson, J. S. (2007). Race, ethnicity, John Henryism, and depressive symptoms: The national survey of American life adult reinterview. *Research in Human Development, 4*(1–2), 71–87.

Smith, W. A., Allen, W. R., & Danley, L. L. (2007). "Assume the position . . . you fit the description" Psychosocial experiences and racial battle fatigue among African American male college students. *American Behavioral Scientist, 51,* 551–578.

CHAPTER 2

THRIVING WHILE BLACK: INSPIRING BLACK MALE EDUCATORS TO GOVERN WITH DIGNITY AND PURPOSE

Black male educators navigate a range of complex challenges in the classroom, where their roles are often overshadowed by stereotypes. Among the most damaging is the perception that they are primarily disciplinarians rather than educators or mentors. This stereotype not only diminishes their professional contributions but also confines them to managing behavior, rather than engaging in meaningful academic or emotional support. The consequences of this limiting view are far-reaching, affecting their interactions with students and colleagues, and the way they perceive their own professional identities. In addition, the portrayal of Black male educators as disciplinarians is deeply entrenched in long-standing racial biases and stereotypes about Black masculinity. Historically, Black men have been unfairly associated with qualities like aggression, authority, and dominance, both in broader society and within educational settings. These stereotypes are damaging and also profoundly shape the way Black male educators are perceived by their peers, students, and school leaders.

The Black Male Educator Guide to Thriving, pages 15–28
Copyright © 2026 by Emerald Publishing Limited
All rights of reproduction in any form reserved.
doi:10.1108/978-1-80592-473-920251003

Within a broader socio-historical context, Black men have often been represented in popular culture and educational research as disciplinary figures, whether as the *tough* Black father in family narratives or the "strict" Black teacher in classrooms. Such portrayals are not only constraining but also fail to recognize the full spectrum of talents, expertise, and teaching philosophies that Black male educators bring to their work. Images such as that of the patriarch on the television show *Good Times* have helped craft the perception of Black males. On the show, John Amos played James Evans, the dutiful husband and father to three children. Situated in the ghetto, the Evans family navigated gang violence, oppressive economic forces, and opportunistic politicians, among other things. Amidst these conditions, James dispensed wisdom and guidance, often reliant on corporal punishment and an authoritative flair. For many, while James was a rigid disciplinarian who offered a harsh denunciation of harmful Black male stereotypes and positivity, other images additionally molded America's ideas of Black men.

For people of a certain age, thinking about Black male educators evokes images of Sidney Poitier in *To Sir, With Love* (Clavell, 1967). In the film, Poitier portrayed Mark Thackeray, a former engineer who, after struggling to find work in his chosen profession, reluctantly takes up a teaching position. At the outset of the film, Thackeray's character is cold, authoritative, and somewhat distant, embodying a persona that reflects many societal expectations of Black male teachers: stern, uncompromising, and emotionally reserved. His brusque demeanor and no-nonsense approach to teaching, particularly in the early stages of the movie, initially alienate the students, leading them to perceive him as harsh and unapproachable. This portrayal taps into the common stereotype that Black male educators are overly strict or even excessively disciplinarian, emphasizing the high expectations placed on them to manage their classrooms with an iron hand. Thackeray's interactions with his students, at first filled with tension and misunderstandings, ultimately challenge this perception as his character softens and grows more empathetic. Over time, his firm but caring approach to teaching demonstrates the complexity and depth that can exist in Black male educators, who, like Thackeray, are often unfairly boxed into limited roles shaped by negative or reductive stereotypes.

For others, Joe Clark, the principal from the movie *Lean on Me* (1989), colors their views of Black male teachers. In this role, Clark, portrayed by Morgan Freeman, is depicted as a tough, no-nonsense educator who takes on the challenge of revitalizing a failing high school in a rough neighborhood. The school is plagued by violence, drug use, and a demoralized faculty, and Clark's primary mission is to restore order and discipline while motivating his students to believe in their potential. His leadership style is unconventional, marked by aggressive tactics and an unwavering commitment to his vision for the school's future. One of the most iconic and controversial symbols of Clark's approach is his frequent wielding of a baseball bat. Although Clark claims the bat was a metaphor, a way to emphasize the choice between "striking out" or "hitting a home run," the image of him holding the bat became deeply ingrained in the public's understanding of his leadership, and by extension, the perceived role of Black male educators.

The bat, with its dual connotation of authority and threat, encapsulates the often-cited stereotype of Black male educators as figures who must maintain control through force and intimidation. The image evokes a broader narrative where Black male teachers are expected to be enforcers of discipline, whose success is measured by their ability to maintain order and assert dominance. Clark's extreme measures, including his confrontation with students and faculty alike, highlight how Black male educators, especially in challenging or underfunded schools, may be viewed as individuals whose value lies in their ability to "tame" their students, using discipline as a tool for improvement. While Clark's character is ultimately portrayed as a hero, someone who turns the school around and pushes students to achieve against all odds, his aggressive methods and the enduring symbol of the baseball bat reveal the tension between the high expectations placed on Black male educators to be both mentors and disciplinarians. This imagery, for many, has become emblematic of a broader societal belief that Black male teachers must be harsh, unyielding, and even confrontational in their roles, reinforcing an ideal of toughness over emotional intelligence or nurturing guidance.

Still others were molded by the striking role of Samuel L. Jackson in the movie *Coach Carter* (2005). Although not a teacher in the traditional sense, Jackson's portrayal of Ken Carter, a high school basketball coach, profoundly influences perceptions of Black male educators. In the film, Carter is a no-nonsense, tough-minded coach who instills discipline, responsibility, and a sense of purpose in his players. His approach is not just about winning basketball games; it's about preparing young men for life beyond the court. Carter demands excellence from his athletes both academically and athletically, setting high standards that extend far beyond sports. His fierce commitment to accountability, coupled with his uncompromising attitude, places him in a role that blends elements of educator, mentor, and disciplinarian, even though his primary title is coach.

All the educators listed above blended high expectations and strong values with love and support. However, the austerity of their dispositions and their firm professional bearing cause many to view them as *mean*, *strict*, and *discipline-focused*. In general, Black men are often perceived as disciplinarians. Bristol and Mentor (2018) highlight that Black male educators often experience the expectation from their colleagues that they should serve primarily as disciplinarians, with teaching and academic support taking a back seat. These educators report that their colleagues typically approach them only for discipline-related concerns and rarely seek their help with curriculum or instructional matters (Bristol & Mentor, 2018).

While Black male educators are demonstrably employed to teach, their roles in traditional school settings often involve much more than just academic instruction. Black males are frequently assigned additional responsibilities, such as addressing the disciplinary issues that arise, particularly challenges faced by Black children.

Contextualizing School Discipline

Fundamental to the notion of school discipline is the more specific area of classroom rules. The concept of classroom *rules* developed from a long history of discipline and social control within educational institutions, particularly as formal education systems grew more structured. Over time, the notion of *rules* in the classroom shifted in response to evolving pedagogical approaches, moving from rigid, authoritarian methods of control to more student-centered practices aimed at promoting positive behavior.

In times past, students who misbehaved were forced to don a dunce cap or they were punished with corporal punishment, often with a belt, a bundle of sticks, or a ruler. Students were also forced to stand for long periods or made to kneel on sharp objects (Doe, 2020). Teachers were given a great deal of discretion to punish students and were regarded as proxies for parents. The Latin phrase in loco parentis provided some educators a wide berth for discipline, and some schools also became purposed with training children how to behave and become good, productive members of society. Racial dynamics have played a significant role in shaping the history of classroom management in the United States, particularly in how Black students have been treated and disciplined. From the earliest days of formal education to the present, Black students have often been subject to disproportionate discipline, racial bias, and the reinforcement of damaging stereotypes. These long-standing patterns in classroom management are deeply intertwined with broader societal systems of racism and inequality, which continue to influence the educational experiences and outcomes of Black students.

Contemporarily, schools have largely eradicated corporal punishment from behavior management approaches and emphasize positive disciplinary measures to encourage and develop healthy behaviors, and exclusionary disciplinary methods. Exclusionary discipline is the practice of removing students from the learning environment, often via suspensions or expulsions from the school context. Disproportionately, Black students are among the populations of students who are subjects of this brand of discipline

(Smith, 2019). Expulsions and suspensions are key factors in the school-to-prison pipeline, contributing to higher rates of youth crime in communities. As zero-tolerance policies become more common for noncriminal behaviors, the context behind the actions that lead to mandatory suspension or expulsion is often ignored (Wirtz, 2021).

Old-School Black Discipline

Concerning discipline, it is vital to explore the way Black people have historically addressed discipline with children. Within the Black family, and depending on the socio-economic standing of the family, there have been an array of techniques used to encourage compliance by Black children. Often fearing that Black children would be hurt by peers, brutalized by police, or flat-out murdered, parents sometimes coerced children to obey the rules of the home and treated them as analogous to laws on the streets. From the time of American slavery onward, Black parents and caregivers have often utilized physical discipline to teach children self-control, hoping to prevent them from drawing the attention and retribution of white authorities. Although many so-called pundits critique Black parents and reduce their diverse parenting style to *whuppins* or other forms of corporal punishment (Adkison-Johnson et al., 2016), there is complexity and strategy often associated with the way Black parents discipline children. Black families have historically varied their approaches to discipline, using strategies ranging from psychological techniques like cautionary and trickster tales to physical punishment, to find the most effective method.

Curiously, Black parents' brand of disciplining their children is often viewed as converse to white parenting styles, leading to increased instances of child abuse cases against Black parents (Luken et al., 2021). And, while researchers have found that corporal punishment is largely ineffective for correcting undesirable behavior, many parents opt for this approach to manage their problems with children for various reasons, including keeping the government out of the family business. Other practices, such as vociferous verbal corrections also emanate from a pronounced fear of out-of-family intervention and have become a regular feature in the homes of many Black people.

In yesteryear, Black parents would have children retrieve a switch, a thin branch from a tree, to spank the child. Alternatively, Black parents would use a belt, an extension cord, or some other implement to encourage compliance. These methods were often passed down through generations and were seen as a way to instill discipline and respect. More often, however, the gesture of a parent can serve as a correction for children. Depending on the gesture, a side eye, a subtle raise of the eyebrow, or a clenching of the jaw can send varying messages to children, signaling disapproval or warning of impending consequences without uttering a word. Verbal admonitions such as "Don't make me come over there" and "This is the last time I am going to tell you…" further represent attempts at correcting wayward behavior, effectively leveraging the power of both nonverbal and verbal cues to maintain order and discipline. These methods, deeply rooted in cultural traditions, reflect both the emotional and strategic ways parents navigate their role in guiding their children's behavior.

Similarly, in the classroom, Black educators have often artfully utilized old-school methods to maintain order. A hand on the hip might suggest that students are talking too much, a stern look may mean that a student should be seated, and an eye roll could indicate that a teacher is at their absolute limit regarding a behavior. These nonverbal cues, though subtle, are powerful forms of communication that carry a weight of cultural understanding. While corporal punishment is disallowed in most public school spaces today, these old-school nonverbal conveyances have transferability from the home to the school, maintaining a link between traditional discipline strategies and modern educational environments. The use of such gestures not only communicates authority but also demonstrates how Black educators navigate their classroom management, fostering a sense of respect and order without the need for harsh physical intervention. Combined with the erroneous, injurious societal constructions of Black males, the broad ideas about how Black parents discipline their children serve as part of the basis for ideas about Black male educators as disciplinarians. These perceptions come at an inordinate cost, however.

Impact of the Disciplinarian Perception

The interactions between Black male educators and their students are often influenced by the same racialized expectations that shape their relationships with colleagues. Research shows that students, especially those from predominantly white or non-Black backgrounds, may perceive Black male educators as more authoritative or intimidating than their white counterparts (Bristol & Mentor, 2018). This perception can lead to a mix of positive and negative outcomes in the classroom.

On the positive side, some students may respect the perceived authority of Black male educators, valuing their ability to maintain discipline and structure, which can create a sense of security in the classroom. On the negative side, however, this focus on discipline can limit the emotional and intellectual support Black male teachers can provide. It can overshadow their capacity to engage with students on a deeper level, addressing both their academic needs and personal growth. Furthermore, when Black male educators are primarily seen as disciplinarians, it can hinder their ability to form nurturing and supportive relationships with students, particularly those who might benefit from positive male role models. This limits students' opportunities to build meaningful, trust-based relationships with their teachers, ultimately affecting their motivation, sense of belonging, and academic performance.

Additionally, the stereotype of Black male educators as disciplinarians can also significantly impact teacher retention and recruitment. Many Black men enter the teaching profession motivated by the desire to make a positive difference in students' lives, aspiring to be both role models and mentors. However, when their professional roles are narrowed to discipline, and their broader contributions go unrecognized, it can lead to disillusionment and burnout.

Studies show that educators who feel their roles are restricted or undervalued are more likely to leave the profession. For Black male educators, this often leads to greater job dissatisfaction and higher turnover rates. Moreover, the enduring stereotype of Black male teachers as strict disciplinarians may deter other potential educators from entering the field, as they may fear being confined to narrow, reductive expectations that do not align with their personal or professional goals. The stereotype of the *angry Black disciplinarian* has long influenced how Black male teachers are perceived, often portraying them as authoritarian or excessively harsh. This damaging narrative not only misrepresents their teaching methods but also limits their ability to create classroom environments where both they and their students can flourish. For Black male educators, thriving goes beyond overcoming classroom challenges; it means creating high-expectation, supportive spaces where students can excel academically and personally. Challenging this stereotype requires dismantling biased assumptions and reframing the role of Black male educators as compassionate leaders who prioritize empathy, student well-being, and academic success. When Black male educators can thrive in their roles, they create classrooms where all students, especially those from marginalized backgrounds, can truly succeed.

Anecdote: *As a K-12 teacher, I would often receive phone calls from my colleagues who would ask for help with their students. Almost invariably, the students sent to me would be Black children, almost always boys. I remember once when a kid, a Black boy, came over from my neighboring teacher's class, he entered with two dictionaries, the old-school thick ones. I asked him why he had two dictionaries and he told me he was supposed to stand in the corner and hold a dictionary in each hand with his arms outstretched. I told him to put down the dictionaries and sit next to me so I could talk to him about a plan for success in his classroom. After the discussion, he commented, "Hey, you're kinda cool. I thought you were mean." When I asked him why he assumed I was mean, he said, "I don't know. I just did."*

Learning to Thrive

Given all of the foregoing information, Black educators and others who work with or supervise Black educators must understand the historical backdrop that undergirds these harmful perceptions. That said, to discuss thriving here partly places the onus on school leaders to shoulder some of the responsibility, however, to thrive, Black males must authentically show up as their natural selves in school spaces. That said, if a teacher is typically mean-spirited, angry, and unfriendly, I would strongly encourage them to change or find a profession better suited to their disposition. After all, we are working with children who are using our disposition as models for how to behave. If a teacher is kind, sweet, and good-natured, they should show up that way in the classroom. Often, new teachers are given admonitions such as *Don't be nice, or they will run over you,* and *Do not smile until after Thanksgiving.* While perhaps well-intentioned, these warnings do little to promote individual authenticity. In fact, I would say these kinds of offerings foster disingenuity and encourage pretension. To thrive, Black male educators have to show up as the person who was reared by their caregivers, as the person who has experienced life as a Black male, and as a person who seeks to promote positive self-identity.

Social Contracts

For Black male educators to thrive, they must work with students to form a shared governance structure in the classroom. As opposed to an authoritarian management style, one rooted in democratic and just principles is more likely to receive buy-in and support from the students. There are numerous examples of this, but one such model would be a classroom that embodies the ideas captured in a *social contract.* From the onset of the school year, Black male educators should openly discuss and negotiate the norms for the classroom space with students to support the construction of a caring and safe environment for students. Additionally, co-constructing classroom norms with students rather than for students empowers and engages students in meaningful ways. Truly, students tend to be more engaged and take greater ownership over their learning and behavior when provided with the opportunity to contribute to the creation of their classroom norms. This process not only ensures that students feel heard, respected, and valued but also creates a critical foundation for cultivating an inclusive and supportive classroom environment where all members can thrive. For Black male educators, this approach to establishing classroom expectations is especially powerful in counteracting the historical marginalization of Black voices in educational spaces. To begin the process, educators must first establish that all voices will be heard and respected before diving into a group brainstorming session on classroom norms. This sets the tone for an open, collaborative, and empowering exchange of ideas.

In these brainstorming sessions, Black male educators serve as facilitators, guiding students through discussions that allow their diverse perspectives to surface. By using affirming and proactive language, educators can help students articulate the core values that will shape their shared classroom space. As Milner (2016) suggests, positive language framing is essential for fostering a classroom environment where students feel empowered and accountable. Black male educators, with their lived experiences and cultural awareness, can leverage their unique positions to not only model effective communication but also help students challenge and disrupt traditional norms that may perpetuate exclusionary practices.

Once these classroom norms have been established, they should be clearly displayed in a prominent location, serving as a visible reminder of the collective commitment to creating a positive, respectful learning environment. Equally important is the involvement of students and parents in the process, with both parties signing the social contract to signify mutual agreement and understanding. This social contract is not a static document but a living, evolving agreement that adapts as the needs of the classroom community shift. By fostering an environment of mutual respect and collaboration, Black male educators can create a dynamic space where all students, particularly those from marginalized groups, can thrive and grow.

Avoiding Injurious Language

Language matters. In educational spaces, the language we use has a profound impact on the tone, culture, and relationships that are fostered. Oftentimes, educators unknowingly rely on terminology that evokes militaristic or authoritarian imagery. Words like "rules," "discipline," "objective," "boot camp," and "direction" are commonly used in schools and classrooms to set expectations and establish order. These terms, however, can unintentionally create an environment that feels rigid, punitive, and even hostile, particularly for Black male educators who may already be stereotyped as enforcers of authority. The language of militarization, words like *drill, deployment*, and *command*, suggests a world of obedience, compliance, and strict control. While some might argue these terms create a sense of structure or discipline, the use of militaristic language can inadvertently perpetuate a culture of dominance and hierarchy. This does not align with the inclusive, supportive, and growth-oriented atmosphere that most educators aspire to create. For students, particularly in diverse classrooms, a more collaborative, nurturing environment can better foster self-confidence, engagement, and positive relationships with both peers and educators.

It is essential, then, for educators, especially Black male educators, to reconsider the language they employ in their classrooms. Rather than relying on words that echo military-style command and control, educators should embrace language that underscores collaboration, kindness, respect, and inclusivity. Words like *expectations, collaboration, communication, partnership,* and *allyship* shift the focus away from domination and toward mutual respect and collective responsibility. For Black male educators, reclaiming the language used in classrooms is vital to shifting the narrative from the stereotypical image of the *Black male disciplinarian* to one of a supportive, nurturing instructional guide and role model.

Black male educators, in particular, need to take control of their language. They should intentionally emphasize terminology that reflects the qualities they wish to impart, those of encouragement, compassion, and mutual respect. When discussions around classroom conduct and student behavior are framed in terms of *expectations* and *collaboration*, Black male educators move away from the authoritarian roles they are sometimes pigeonholed into and towards more positive, empathetic positions. Rather than being seen as disciplinarians, these educators can be viewed as facilitators of personal growth and educational success, helping students to develop both academically and personally. Small yet significant changes in language can thus dismantle the stereotypical *enforcer* image and elevate Black male educators as pillars of support and guidance in the classroom.

This collaborative approach to behavior management signals a shift away from *rules* imposed from above to a more egalitarian and nurturing classroom culture. Educators should work with students to create and maintain this list of agreed-upon expectations, which will be framed not in terms of punishment or control, but in the spirit of cooperation and shared responsibility.

To disrupt this outdated paradigm, Black male educators should move away from using the term *rules* and instead adopt terms like *classroom behavior standards, classroom expectations*, or *behavior expectations*. These alternatives imply a shared responsibility for creating a positive, respectful environment and are less likely to evoke the rigid, authoritarian tone of military-style discipline. Furthermore, behavior expectations should not be seen as a list of imposed regulations, but rather as an evolving social contract that students and educators create together. In doing so, the classroom becomes a space where students feel empowered to take ownership of their behavior, as opposed to one where they are merely complying with imposed restrictions.

When the language used in classrooms reflects collaboration and esprit de corps, a sense of mutual respect and collective responsibility, there is less room for the authoritarian imagery associated with traditional notions of discipline. Instead, the emphasis shifts to growth, learning, and community.

As Black male educators, embracing this shift in language not only helps dismantle harmful stereotypes but also creates a more inclusive, nurturing environment where all students can thrive. In turn, this helps Black male educators to break free from the *disciplinarian* role and more fully embody their positions as guides, nurturers, and models of decency, whose influence is grounded in care, support, and positive engagement.

Personal Storytelling: Bringing Lived Experiences Into the Classroom

Personal storytelling is a potent tool for Black male educators to create a deeper connection with their students and to infuse their classrooms with authenticity. Sharing personal stories about how your upbringing, cultural background, and life experiences shape your perspective on education can not only humanize you as a teacher but also make the learning experience more relatable for students. For instance, educators could share how growing up in a specific community or family environment shaped their understanding of perseverance, success, or identity. This might involve reflecting on the values instilled by your caregivers, such as resilience, pride, or the importance of education, and how those values influence your teaching approach today. Other stories could also highlight challenges you faced, whether they were related to race, socio-economic background, or personal setbacks, and how overcoming those challenges has shaped the way you engage with students. For example, you might share how experiencing hardship early in life led you to believe in the power of education as a tool for upward mobility, or how an influential teacher, mentor, or family member inspired you to become an educator. These stories do not need to be dramatic or traumatic; often, it's the simple, everyday moments of growth and learning that resonate the most with students. The goal is to communicate that your life experiences have equipped you to understand their struggles, guide their development, and support them as they navigate their journeys.

For example, you might say:

> When I was growing up, my mom always told me that education would be the key to unlocking opportunities for me. She wasn't wrong. I remember struggling in school sometimes, and it was the teachers who saw me for who I was, not just as a student, but as a person, that made the biggest difference. They helped me realize that my background, my experiences, and my culture weren't obstacles but strengths. I want to do the same for you, to show you how your unique story can help you succeed.

Storytelling builds an authentic connection between the educator and students. When Black male educators share personal experiences, students can see reflections of their own lives in the narrative, which fosters a sense of relatability and mutual understanding. This connection is important because it moves the teacher from being just an authority figure to someone who can be trusted, understood, and approached for support. Students are more likely to feel valued and heard when they know their teacher has lived through experiences that align with their own. It shows students that their struggles are not isolated; they are part of a larger, shared human experience.

Furthermore, by sharing personal stories, Black male educators model vulnerability and authenticity, qualities that are essential for building trust in the classroom. When students hear their teacher talk about their own challenges, growth, and successes, it creates an environment where students feel safer to express themselves and take risks in their learning. These stories also offer students hope and inspiration, as they see that someone who has faced similar challenges has not only survived but thrived. This can be especially empowering for Black students, who may see their teacher's success as a blueprint for their own potential.

In addition, personal storytelling allows Black male educators to challenge harmful stereotypes. It disrupts the narrow view of Black men as *strict disciplinarians* or *angry figures* by offering a fuller, more nuanced picture of their identities. By sharing stories that show their complexity, compassion, and depth, Black male educators can break down these stereotypes and present themselves as supportive role models who are invested in the success of all students. This approach makes it clear to students that their teacher's life experiences are intertwined with the subjects they teach, making education feel less abstract and more grounded in real-world applications.

In practice, personal storytelling can be incorporated into daily classroom activities, whether through formal lessons, informal discussions, or one-on-one conversations. By weaving personal experiences into the fabric of teaching, educators encourage students to reflect on their own journeys, creating an environment where stories, both personal and collective, are valued and shared. This kind of interaction cultivates a classroom community built on trust, respect, and shared learning.

Ultimately, personal storytelling is a powerful tool that allows Black male educators to create an inclusive, supportive, and authentic classroom environment. When educators share their own experiences, they not only build stronger relationships with their students but also provide them with valuable lessons about resilience, identity, and the importance of seeing oneself reflected in the world.

Conclusion

When Black male educators successfully navigate the discipline label, they not only alter how they are perceived but also have a profound, positive impact on their students' learning experiences. By fostering environments that blend authority with compassion, they encourage student participation, build self-esteem, and help cultivate a healthy racial identity. Through mentorship that extends beyond academics, Black male educators provide students with the tools to navigate the complexities of their personal and social identities. Additionally, they challenge harmful stereotypes, demonstrating that Black male educators are multifaceted leaders who play a critical role in shaping their students' holistic development.

Overcoming the discipline label requires perseverance, self-awareness, and a steadfast commitment to promoting inclusion. By confronting the racially problematic stereotypes discussed in this chapter, Black male educators help transform their classrooms and contribute to reshaping the broader educational landscape, ensuring it is a more inclusive, supportive, and empowering space where all students can thrive and develop a strong, healthy sense of self.

To Thrive, Black male educators should:

1. Develop a Social Contract with the Students
2. Avoid Injurious language
3. Using Personal Storytelling to Bring Lived Experiences into the Classroom

Questions for Reflection

1. How do you develop classroom expectations?
2. As the teacher, do you hold yourself to account for infractions of those expectations?
3. How do you navigate the stereotypes associated with Black male teachers, and can you challenge or reshape these perceptions in the classroom and within the broader school community?

References

Adkison-Johnson, C., Terpstra, J., Burgos, J., & Payne, E. D. (2016). African American child discipline: Differences between mothers and fathers. *Family Court Review, 54*(2), 203–220.

Bristol, T. J., & Mentor, M. (2018). Policing and teaching: The positioning of Black male teachers as agents in the universal carceral apparatus. *The Urban Review, 50*, 218–234.

Clavell, J. (Director). (1967). *To Sir, with Love* [Film]. Columbia Pictures.

Doe, J. (2020). *The history of education and punishment.* Education Press.

Luken, A., Nair, R., & Fix, R. L. (2021). On racial disparities in child abuse reports: Exploratory mapping the 2018 NCANDS. *Child Maltreatment, 26*(3), 267–281.

Milner, H. R. (2016). A Black male teacher's culturally responsive practices. *The Journal of Negro Education, 85*(4), 417–432. https://doi.org/10.7709/jnegroeducation.85.4.0417

Smith, J. (2019). *Discipline in education: A history of racial disparities.* Education Press.

Wirtz, A. (2021). Zero-tolerance policies and their impact on student discipline. *Journal of Educational Policy, 32*(3), 45–59.

CHAPTER 3

TO SIR, WITH LOVE: HOW BLACK MALE EDUCATORS FOSTER THRIVING RELATIONSHIPS

In general, teacher relationships with peers in a school setting can be richly rewarding or damning from the outset. For Black male educators, relationships are even more pronounced, in part because of the comparably few Black males in educational spaces, and also due to rampant anti-Blackness. The way a Black male educator moves concerning teacher colleagues, administrators, caregivers, and other school personnel can have impactful repercussions, so careful deliberation must be employed in navigating each relationship. Importantly, Black males should be attuned to the implicit and explicit biases they may encounter, ensuring they are balancing professionalism with personal identity. The educator's reputation and approach to relationship-building can set the tone for how they are perceived and treated within the school community. It is also important to note that society's perception of the Black male educator has been shaped by popular media, which has tended to conceive of Black males in a certain light.

A poignant example of this can be seen in the film *To Sir, With Love* (Clavell, 1967), where Sidney Poitier's character, Mark Thackeray, navigates his role as a Black male teacher in a classroom of unruly students in London. Thackeray faces skepticism and prejudice from both students and fellow educators due to his race and lack of experience. However, Thackeray's approach to relationship-building is both deliberate and strategic. By setting high expectations for his students and showing them respect, he breaks down the barriers of mistrust and disdain that the students initially have toward him. His relationships with his students are complex; he isn't simply an authority figure, but a mentor who shows empathy and patience while simultaneously asserting his authority. Thackeray's relationship with his peers and administrators also shifts as they witness his ability to connect with the students and achieve meaningful change. This dynamic highlights how Black male educators, through intentional communication, respect, and understanding, can forge impactful relationships that positively influence their teaching environment. Just as Thackeray balances professional boundaries with human connection, Black male educators must carefully navigate their roles to ensure they are seen as both authoritative and relatable, despite the challenges they may face.

Yes, relationships are vital for a Black male educator to thrive. Yet, not all educators have the disposition, physical attributes, etc. of Mark Thackerary (Sidney Poitier), and it is especially important that Black males develop a healthy sense of their own identities to fare well in school spaces. While Thackeray is an inspiring figure, his character embodies qualities that are not always easily replicated. His composed, almost paternalistic attitude, paired with his undeniable physical presence, represents an ideal of teaching that may feel out of reach for many Black male educators who do not fit this particular mold. Thackeray's persona is built upon a combination of a clear moral compass, emotional intelligence, and personal authority, all of which are essential traits for effective teaching. However, this representation often creates unrealistic expectations for Black male educators, who may feel that they need to embody this same *perfect teacher* archetype to succeed. The pressure to meet these expectations can be particularly overwhelming when considering the historical and societal stereotypes that Black male educators often face, such as being perceived as authoritarian or disciplinarians rather than compassionate or nurturing figures.

Perhaps most insidious is that Black male educators are often expected to navigate these stereotypes while simultaneously meeting the complex needs of their students. The myth of the *Black male disciplinarian* casts a long shadow over their profession, placing disproportionate pressure on them to take on roles that emphasize control and authority, rather than support and mentorship. Black male educators, who are often expected to exert discipline and command order, are at risk of being pigeonholed into enforcer roles rather than being seen as guides and mentors who facilitate holistic student development. This expectation for Black male educators to adopt a strict, no-nonsense persona can be restrictive and may not align with the diverse, multifaceted identities that they bring to their teaching roles.

Relationships With Teacher Colleagues

While it is the case that Black males develop wonderful and long-lasting friendships and working relationships with teacher colleagues, there are also enough converse reports to merit exploration here. The professional relationships that Black male teachers have with their teacher colleagues are often shaped by intersecting race and gender dynamics, which can complicate their experiences in predominantly white teacher settings. Amid the numerous issues reported by Black male educators, many shared feelings of marginalization, encountering microaggressions, or enduring stereotypes that question their teaching abilities or character (Sleeter, 2011). Often, non-white teacher colleagues form relationships that exclude Black male educators, and because there are relatively few Black people in educational spaces, a palpable isolation results. Further, relationships with teacher colleagues are a strong predictor of whether Black males remain in the field (Sandles, 2018), change school placements, or withdraw from connectivity with adult school personnel. Importantly, there are dimensions of social connectivity with teacher colleagues that warrant discussion.

Sexual Harassment

An underreported aspect of the Black male educator's experience is sexual harassment. This form of hostility can present as comments about a Black male teacher's body, propositioning Black male educators for sexual favors, constant flirtation with Black males, and physical touching of their bodies. These behaviors can regularly impact the professional relationships of Black male teachers with their colleagues. For Black male teachers, the added layers of racial and gendered stereotyping can exacerbate feelings of isolation, leaving them with limited avenues for support. Moreover, the *hypermasculine* stereotype often imposed on Black men, associating them with aggression, sexual dominance, and emotional stoicism, can significantly disrupt professional dynamics in the workplace (Collins, 2004). These deeply ingrained racialized perceptions shape how Black male teachers are viewed and interacted with by colleagues, particularly female staff members. In such environments, these teachers may find themselves subjected to assumptions about their sexuality, with their actions misinterpreted as either threatening or flirtatious. This not only creates uncomfortable or inappropriate interactions but also places Black male teachers in the difficult position of constantly navigating and dismantling these damaging stereotypes, which can undermine their professional authority and emotional well-being.

Black men in general are frequently depicted in media and popular culture as hypersexual beings, driven by a primal sexual desire and aggression. This stereotype of the oversexed Black man is deeply rooted in historical tropes that have long painted Black men as sexually dangerous, threatening, and uncontrollable. In the educational context, these stereotypes can manifest in uncomfortable and inappropriate ways. Black male teachers may find themselves the subject of uninvited advances or comments from female colleagues who, influenced by the stereotype of the hypersexual Black man, may interpret a teacher's presence, demeanor, or even body language as flirtatious or suggestive. These advances, often in the form of inappropriate compliments or physical touch, can create an emotionally charged work environment in which Black male teachers feel objectified or disrespected.

> **Anecdote**: *Following a very productive planning session with several female colleagues, a few of them began to leave my classroom, the site of the meeting. One of my colleagues, a white female with whom I struck up a friendship, leaned over and kissed me on the head. She then smiled at me and rubbed my arm up and down, making me feel violated and incredibly uncomfortable. As a married man whose wife and children had visited the school often, I felt incredibly awkward and even more uncertain about how to move forward. My wife, a Black woman, was pissed and understandably wanted to pursue a violent recourse. However, cooler heads prevailed, and we decided I would report the incident to the site principal. The principal, also a white woman, was supportive and understanding, and she assured me she would address the matter, which she did. Unfortunately, the aftermath of the report had ramifications, as the perpetrator began to spread stories about me being a tease, and many of my other colleagues immediately stopped speaking to me. After speaking with other Black male educators and reading the literature on Black male teachers, I learned that experiences of this kind were not uncommon.*

When sexual harassment is unacknowledged or brushed off by school leadership, it contributes to a toxic culture where harassment becomes normalized and overlooked. Black male teachers may feel unable to report harassment, fearing that doing so could lead to further racialization of their behavior or result in professional isolation. The intersection of racial and gendered stereotypes often leaves Black male teachers in a precarious position where their credibility and authority are questioned, and their experiences of harassment are invalidated or minimized. Adding on, there is another popular and equally toxic experience Black male educators endure.

Gossip Groups

A potential landmine for Black male educators is the teacher's lounge. Ostensibly, it is more than just a physical space; it is a vital retreat where educators gather outside of class hours to recharge and connect. Amid their demanding schedules, it offers a rare opportunity for relaxation, conversation, and collaboration with colleagues. It serves as both a sanctuary, offering a break from the intensity of classroom life, and a hub for professional exchange. Additionally, the teacher's lounge can cultivate a sense of community, foster collegiality, and develop shared understandings among educators. In this way, the teacher's lounge plays an essential role in sustaining both the well-being and professional growth of educators. However, the teacher's lounge can also serve as a venue for vitriol.

The teacher's lounge often also represents a place where many disgruntled educators go to vent their frustrations. Wayward students, irate parents, curriculum changes, and gripes about site administration are frequently the topics of discussion; however, in some instances, no one is safe from the possibility of being ridiculed. The teacher's lounge and other spaces present fair game to colleagues to unbraid anyone who has ventured into their crosshairs. The teacher's lounge can be a place of refuge for many teachers, but Black male educators should be wary of toxic lounges and should pay attention to groups and discussions that otherwise demonize people, places, and things. The worst kind of demonization, in my view, is that of students, so colleagues who spew hurtful comments about students, comments that disparage a child's physical characteristics, their speech patterns, their clothing, etc., should be avoided.

Anecdote: *My first year teaching was an adventure for many reasons. As a Black male, I had heard about the teacher's lounge and how dispiriting it can be. However, I wanted to be hopeful and gave it a chance. When I entered, there were three groups of teachers and staff members situated at different tables. One table was laughing and talking about something I could not make out, another table was talking about a teacher who was constantly absent, and my table was discussing a student. "Her hair stinks," one of them said. Her mom needs to wash it, like every single day. The female teacher then turns to me and says, "No disrespect, but can Black people wash their hair everyday? I don't really know." Stuck, and not wanting to provide additional fodder for discussion, I simply said, "Yes." At that point, another female staff person from a different table joined in our discussion. "How long does it take to braid that hair?" she wondered aloud. "Can they take it down, wash it, and braid it fairly quickly?" I shrugged my shoulders to indicate my uncertainty and left it at that, cognizant that whatever I said in that moment could render me a friend or foe to the group. Finally, another female teacher said, "I had her sister for the afternoon class, and her hair smelled the same way. I usually just opened the window when she came in." As the only*

> Black person present and one of two Black educators in the school, I was unsure of how to navigate this experience.

Gossip groups can ostracize, belittle, and undermine various personnel on campus, so it is important to be cognizant of them once they start to form. Plus, Black males who participate in these groups will often become the face of the comments when other share what was said. In other words, the gossip will often be attributed to the Black male teacher rather than its rightful source.

Relationships With School Administration

The relationship between Black male teachers and school administrators is often shaped by issues of authority, race, and representation. Research indicates that Black male teachers are sometimes perceived as either too authoritative or too lenient, depending on the racialized expectations placed upon them by school leaders. Administrators may struggle to understand the unique experiences and challenges faced by Black male educators, which can lead to a lack of support and opportunities for professional advancement.

Building and maintaining a positive relationship with school leaders is essential for several reasons. Whether their title is principal, director, or head of school, administrators are the primary decision-makers within a school, setting the tone for the school's culture, discipline policies, and academic priorities. For Black male educators, developing a strong relationship with the principal can be a source of professional empowerment, emotional support, and career advancement. Navigating successful relationships with site administration can be tricky and sometimes perilous, depending on the moves one makes. While a professional distance is probably advantageous, it is also beneficial to work professionally close to the site administration so that needed resources and general support can be procured. In particular, the professional development, assistance with student supporting students, and resource allocation are conspicuous opportunities that may be afforded Black male educators through positive relations with school leadership.

Because site administrators are often responsible for mentoring teachers, offering professional development opportunities, and providing resources, it is vital to maintain a strong, positive connection with them, as a positive relationship ensures that a Black male educator can access these opportunities for growth and success. When conferences or other professional learning opportunities are available on a topic of interest, it is often the site administrator who approves them, so intact relationships help this cause. This might include access to specialized leadership training, opportunities to work on district-wide committees, or mentorship for pursuing advanced degrees or certifications. Site administrators who recognize the value of investing in their staff's growth are more likely to provide the resources and encouragement necessary to help Black male educators achieve their career goals. A related aspect of this benefit is that new teachers develop their beginning teacher identity through positive connections with the site administrators. Black male educators can literally sculpt the way they see the profession in general and their own professional bearing by learning from site administrators.

Further, strong connections with site administrators can assist Black male educators in disrupting school policies that are often disproportionately punitive for Black students, particularly Black male students, and can contribute to the school-to-prison pipeline (Bristol & Mentor, 2018). Black male educators, who are in a unique position to relate to these students, can work alongside the principal to advocate for restorative justice practices and alternative discipline models that prioritize rehabilitation and equity. Building a strong rapport with the principal means that Black male educators can influence these policies and practices to better serve the needs of their students.

Site administrators also figure noticeably in determining how resources are allocated within the school. Black male educators who develop and cultivate strong relationships with site administrators can advocate for the distribution of resources in ways that directly benefit students needing academic support, those who require mentorship, and extracurricular activities that support students. For example, the educator may advocate for funding for athletics or chess programs that engage Black male students or for specialized tutoring services for those struggling academically. The benefits mentioned above greatly support Black male educators and add to their catalogs of experiences and ability to perform well in the classroom. However, it is often the case that when a Black male educator speaks out of turn or otherwise runs afoul of a site administrator, the human and financial resources that are generally available become inaccessible.

Anecdote: *I had a fantastic relationship with my school principal at first. The first couple of years were great. I could go to her about anything and received a lot of support. At first. Then, I spoke up in a staff meeting about funding for a debate club I started. I wanted to know when we were going to receive the monies promised to finance our trips and competitions. Without trying to, I know I made her look kind of bad, but I had not gotten any answers to my questions via email, so I wanted to take action. Well, after that, she would come into my classroom many times per week demanding to see my lesson plans, whereas before she almost never came in. She would leave me notes about what she observed during her classroom walkthroughs, and although the first item or two were positive, there was a laundry list of things I had done poorly. This happened maybe three or four times each week. I asked other teachers if the principal was visiting them as often and everyone I asked said that she never visited them. The straw that broke the camel's back was when she decided to put another teacher in charge of the debate club I created! Her rationale was that the other teacher had more experience with such projects and had*

> better relationships with our partner schools. I complained to the district, but they found that nothing the principal had done was retaliatory and was all within her purview as the school leader. I knew it was time to leave the school, so I voluntarily transferred at the end of the year.

Moreover, Black male teachers may be subject to disproportionate disciplinary actions or microaggressions from administrators, particularly in schools where racial diversity is minimal. These educators may also feel pressure to conform to the expectations of their administrators, which often align with traditional, Eurocentric standards of professionalism. In some cases, administrators' failure to provide adequate support for Black male teachers can contribute to high levels of burnout and turnover. Regrettably, it is a common experience for educators to become ensnared in school politics and to find themselves at odds with the site administrators. Given the confluence of race, gender, and the oftentimes accompanying perceptions of Black male educators, relations between site administrators and Black males must be positive or at least workable.

Parent involvement

Often overlooked and misused stakeholders in the process of helping Black male educators thrive are parents and caregivers. I use the term *caregiver collaborations* as distinct from *parent engagement* or *parent involvement* because, to me, those terms do not go far enough to represent the partnership between home and school. And, not all those who care for children are parents. Additionally, educators should not want caregivers to be simply engaged and involved in the partnership, but educators should advocate that caregivers be essential architects and executioners of the work to be done. Although many districts will excitedly tout parent engagement as a core initiative, it is an undergirding principle for Black male educator success that caregiver collaborations feature prominently. Establishing strong, supportive relationships with caregivers, whether they are parents, guardians, or extended family members, is a cornerstone of student success. For Black male educators, this collaboration can have a particularly powerful impact, not only on individual students' academic outcomes but also on their emotional well-being and cultural identity. And, Black male teachers are uniquely positioned to bridge the gap between home and school, leveraging their shared cultural experiences to create a meaningful connection with families. Through these relationships, educators can build a holistic support system for students that extends beyond the classroom.

Moreover, Black male teachers often face challenges in proving their competence to parents, who may harbor strong feelings about the educational system's treatment of Black children. For perspective, calls to end cultural competency, positive rewards, and equity are under attack and deemed to help *only* students of color. However, when these teachers engage in culturally responsive teaching and demonstrate a genuine commitment to their students' success, they can build strong, trust-based relationships with parents. This connection is particularly important in communities where families face systemic inequities and marginalization. For many Black caregivers, the desire to collaborate with educators is a frightening proposition since their own experiences with school might have been harrowing and uncomfortable. Black male educators can build a deeper understanding of the unique challenges their students may face by engaging with their caregivers. These challenges could range from navigating cultural identity in a predominantly white school setting to dealing with social and economic pressures at home.

Having caregivers as active partners provides invaluable insight into these issues, allowing educators to adapt their teaching strategies and interventions accordingly. To bridge the divide between school and home, these collaborations are essential. Black male teachers who share cultural experiences with families can ensure that students' cultural backgrounds are reflected in the curriculum, classroom practices, and school events, creating a learning environment that feels affirming rather than alienating (Louque & Latunde, 2014).

Many Black families harbor a deep mistrust of educational institutions due to a long history of inequitable treatment and strained relationships. This mistrust is rooted in the historical legacy of exclusion, marginalization, and the systemic bias that has often characterized the interactions between Black families and schools. For many Black families, the narratives presented by teachers, principals, and school staff, often portraying them as passive, disengaged, or uninterested in their children's education, are not only inaccurate but dismissive of the real challenges they face. This misrepresentation exacerbates existing tensions and frustrates efforts to build trust and cooperation.

Black male educators play a critical role in helping Black parents feel more confident and empowered in their involvement in their children's education. For many Black parents, navigating the school system can be a daunting experience, one that often feels disconnected from their lived realities or sometimes even dismissive of their concerns. Black male educators, through shared cultural experiences, can bridge these gaps by providing parents with practical tools and strategies to actively advocate for their children's academic success. In part, this could include demystifying the educational system, explaining how to interpret standardized test scores or school assessments, and offering guidance on how to navigate parent-teacher conferences effectively. Beyond the mechanics of school systems, these educators can also equip parents with strategies for supporting their child's emotional and intellectual development at home.

Anecdote: *I remember when I was in my third or fourth year of teaching and I started working really closely with parents to have them in my classroom more. I would have them come in and lead reading groups or prepare homework packets, things like that. One day, I was talking to a parent and she told me that she tried to avoid going through the office. When I asked her the reason, she said that they (office staff) made her feel unwelcome. She told me she did not finish high school and felt like the way the office staff spoke to her indicated they were superior. She felt constantly put down. To cope, she would sometimes sneak through the back gate to visit her daughter's classroom, hoping to avoid the secretary and the other office staff. One time, she was caught without a visitor's pass and said she felt like a criminal.*

Ultimately, the goal is not just to address immediate concerns but to cultivate a long-term partnership between Black parents and the school system, one rooted in mutual trust, understanding, and a shared commitment to student success. Given some of the enumerated challenges, Black male educators can serve as important conduits and interpreters of information and advocates for Black parents who need support within school structures.

Learning to Thrive

One of the most powerful ways Black male educators can thrive within the administrative structure is by being vocal advocates for equitable practices. Whether it's pushing for more culturally relevant curricula, addressing disparities in school discipline, or advocating for resources for underrepresented students, standing up for what students need helps position Black males as essential voices within the school structure. By making equity a central part of advocacy, Black male educators can inspire meaningful change and build positive rapport with administrators who are committed to improving the educational experience for all. In particular, Black males can utilize the techniques below to thrive in their relationships with school administrators.

Open, Regular Communication

Black male educators can thrive by being proactive in sharing updates about student progress, classroom needs, and any obstacles they are encountering. There should be care taken not to overshare personal circumstances, but professional barriers that prevent the attainment of positive student outcomes need to be communicated. For example, if students require access to blocked websites, technological hardware, and textbooks, Black male educators should reach out to the administrator or their designee for access to resources. This can also be achieved by scheduling standing meetings with site administration to share updates and needs. This proactive approach shows administrators the investment in their students' well-being and a commitment to improving the learning environment. Additionally, most school employees have little contact with Black men in professional learning spaces, so high-level, transparent communication with administrators brings about a certain level of education for them, providing rich engagement with Black men in an educational environment.

Thriving within an educational institution often also means cultivating alliances with key stakeholders, particularly those in administrative roles who can amplify their voices. Black male educators can benefit from seeking out mentors or allies in positions of power, people who understand the challenges of navigating race and institutional dynamics. These alliances can provide invaluable support, amplify the educator's concerns, and push for changes that are in the best interest of students and staff alike. In any workplace, power dynamics exist, and Black male educators often face subtle and sometimes overt challenges related to race and authority. Thriving in this space requires not only being attuned to these dynamics but also knowing when to assert yourself diplomatically or when to advocate for necessary changes.

Addressing Sexual Harassment

Sexual harassment in any form is a serious issue that no educator should face alone. For Black male educators, the complexities of addressing sexual harassment can be compounded by gender and racial dynamics. Navigating these situations requires a combination of knowledge, emotional intelligence, and institutional support. Consequently, Black male educators should know the district's policies and procedures regarding sexual harassment, as thriving in the face of sexual harassment starts with being fully apprised of this information. Black male educators must familiarize themselves with how to report incidents, protect students, and hold others accountable when these issues arise. Therefore, an earnest investigation into where policies and reporting procedures can be procured is critically important. Often, human resources departments will have all the needed information, but if Black male teachers are uncomfortable seeking resources from official channels such as human resources, a trusted colleague might also have access to this information, or they might be willing to retrieve it. Because these situations are sensitive and uncomfortable, a reliance on support systems can be incredibly beneficial. Support networks could include colleagues, administrators, or union representatives who can help navigate these difficult conditions. If available, a veteran Black male mentor can serve as a strong guide and advisor through the process, providing insights from both a professional and cultural perspective.

Moreover, Black male educators must recognize the unique psychological toll that sexual harassment can take, particularly in environments where race and gender intersect to influence how their concerns may be perceived or dismissed. Being a Black male educator might sometimes lead others to invalidate or downplay experiences with harassment, assuming the Black male might be tougher than most due to racial stereotypes. Such assumptions make it even more important to document incidents carefully and seek support from those who understand both the emotional and professional challenges these educators face.

In general, research indicates that these collaborative environments promote not only job satisfaction but also improved student outcomes (Villegas & Lucas, 2004). They may be especially beneficial in instances of sexual harassment, as such networks not only provide necessary emotional and institutional support but also foster a sense of solidarity and empowerment. Building such a network, however, is a proactive step that should be undertaken early, long before a crisis occurs, to ensure that a teacher's experience and perspective are respected and validated in all professional contexts. Ultimately, the goal should be to create a school environment where all educators, particularly Black male educators, can thrive and feel safe from harassment, while also maintaining a clear understanding of the avenues for support available to them.

Addressing Gossip Groups

Gossip can be a corrosive force in any workplace, and Black male educators may be particularly vulnerable to gossip that hinges on racial or gender-based stereotypes. These educators can often find themselves the subject of negative talk, which can be compounded by preexisting biases and misconceptions about Black men in professional spaces. However, it's possible to thrive in such environments by developing self-awareness, maintaining professionalism, and creating a network of support. One of the most effective ways to navigate gossip is to avoid engaging in it altogether. Thriving in this environment requires emotional discipline. By not participating in negative conversations or rumor mills, Black males demonstrate integrity and set a positive example for others. This helps maintain focus on professional work and students, rather than getting caught up in office politics or toxic dynamics.

Literally walking away from disparaging discussions can be an effective technique for addressing them. When Black male educators take the initiative to remove themselves from gossip-filled situations, they send a strong message about their values and commitment to fostering a positive school culture. An effective approach may be to employ *escape words*—phrases such as "I need to enter student grades" or "I need to return a parent phone call," which allow for relatively safe evasion of gossip groups without drawing unwanted attention or creating conflict. These strategies, while simple, can serve as vital tools for disengagement and maintaining professional boundaries. Over time, others will perceive Black male educators as those who are unwilling to participate in these conversations, and the inclination to gossip may hopefully subside.

Building emotional resilience and strengthening the ability to stay calm amidst gossip is critical to professional growth. When faced with rumors or negative discussions, Black male educators can consciously redirect their energy towards reinforcing their positive contributions in the classroom, focusing on student success, and relying on their support network for encouragement. Maintaining this mindset helps to preserve their sense of purpose and keep the distractions of gossip at bay. Support networks, whether composed of mentors, trusted colleagues, or professional organizations, provide essential emotional support, perspective, and practical advice. These networks serve as invaluable resources, helping Black male educators stay grounded and focused on their mission, despite the challenges they may face.

By consistently avoiding negative conversations, modeling positive behavior, and fostering inclusive environments, they can shift the atmosphere in their schools. This creates a culture where gossip loses its power and professional conduct is valued. In the long run, these intentional actions contribute to a healthier workplace where educators feel supported, respected, and empowered to thrive.

Direct Communication

If you become the subject of gossip, confronting it directly, calmly, and professionally can often shut it down. However, one does need to be mindful that images of the angry Black male constantly loom, so a professional approach is essential with this method. It is also advisable to have another person in attendance if opting for this method. Communication that begins with *May I please speak with you about a sensitive matter* can open the door to a respectful discussion, allowing the conversation to remain focused on the issue rather than emotions. Additionally, it is advisable not to be confrontational if you state your case and the party argues with your information. While the information presented should be fact-based, the party may still argue or disagree. If so, the Black male educator should politely end the discussion with terminology such as *Thank you for your time* or *I appreciate you for meeting with me*. This helps to maintain composure and professionalism while avoiding unnecessary escalation.

It vitally important to remember that some individuals may be resistant to acknowledging the issue at hand, and in such cases, gracefully disengaging can prevent further complications. After the conversation, consult with your witness to ensure that their recollection aligns with yours. It is equally important to document in writing what occurred during the discussion, noting any key points, responses, or behaviors that might serve as evidence later. This documentation not only protects you but also creates a record in case the situation escalates or resurfaces. If the situation persists or the gossip continues, this written record becomes invaluable for reporting the issue to the appropriate authorities, such as human resources or administration. In these instances, maintaining a calm, well-documented response can demonstrate professionalism and a commitment to resolving the issue constructively, ensuring that any harmful gossip is addressed appropriately. Approaching those involved with the facts and directly addressing the issue not only can possibly defuse rumors set the tone for open communication and accountability. By confronting gossip constructively, you establish boundaries and protect your professional reputation.

Caregiver Collaborations

Collaboration with caregivers is a key component of a thriving educational experience for students, and Black male educators have a unique opportunity to strengthen these partnerships. Engaging with families from a place of empathy, cultural understanding, and transparency can create lasting bonds that positively impact student success. These connections allow Black male educators to not only support academic achievement but also address emotional and social needs, creating a more holistic learning environment. By fostering open communication with caregivers, educators can gain valuable insights into students' home lives, which can inform teaching strategies and better meet individual needs.

Black male educators can also thrive by recognizing that families are not monolithic. In any community, there are diverse backgrounds, experiences, and challenges that may shape how caregivers engage with the educational system. For example, some families may have strong prior experiences with school involvement, while others may feel disconnected or apprehensive due to past negative interactions or systemic barriers. Being sensitive to these differences and adjusting outreach efforts accordingly ensures that all families feel welcomed and supported. This might involve offering multiple communication avenues, such as emails, phone calls, or even virtual meetings, to ensure caregivers feel comfortable participating. Additionally, showing respect for cultural values and traditions while also addressing academic and behavioral expectations can help bridge any gaps between home and school.

Information, Workshops, and Support Groups

Thriving as a Black male educator also means empowering caregivers with the tools they need to support their children. I would advise meeting with caregivers to learn their preferred communication medium. Some favor phone communication, while others value text messages or classroom applications such as *Class Dojo*. Acquiring this information will enable Black male educators to increase the possibility of connecting with caregivers and it communicates a genuine concern for the caregiver's preferences. Once the connection is established, it is important to survey the caregivers to learn what information would be most valuable to them for workshops or support groups. Because there will likely be various cultures represented in classroom spaces, capturing these voices and needs is incredibly useful. A five-item Google survey created in multiple languages can help Black male educators understand the population they are serving and can assist in the design of caregiver connections. See the sample below:

1. What are the best days/times to contact you?
2. How would you prefer to receive information from the school about your child's progress and school events?
3. What challenges or concerns do you feel you need more support with as a parent in helping your child succeed in school?
4. How comfortable do you feel reaching out to the teacher(s) for support or questions?
5. How can the school better support your family's cultural or community needs?

Irrespective of grade level, the questions above can galvanize the collaborative process with caregivers. Importantly, it is important to connect with Black parents, who often harbor distrust toward schools and institutions (Louque & Latunde, 2014), to offer additional and flexible support. Assurances that their child's best interests are the chief concern and consistent follow-up demonstrate that focus is an effective method for garnering support from Black parents.

Additionally, in my experience, caregivers often seek information surrounding homework support, assistance with setting behavioral parameters, and guidance regarding special education considerations. Black male educators will likely be relied upon to assist with behavioral support, as they often fill a surrogate fatherhood role. It is always advisable to remain professional and share advice *only* based on current and accessible research. If enough caregivers express interest in learning about thematic content, educators can share the information broadly via email, caregiver newsletter, or support group to disseminate the material. By organizing information, workshops, or support groups, whether focused on academic skills, mental health, or navigating the school system, Black male educators create opportunities for caregivers to gain knowledge, connect, and feel more confident in their role.

Additionally, for caregivers to partner meaningfully, they need to trust that their child's teacher is transparent and communicative. Black male educators can thrive by being proactive in sharing student progress, addressing any challenges, and offering solutions in a clear, consistent manner. This openness helps caregivers feel more connected to their child's education, knowing they are part of a collaborative team. This information should also be shared with caregivers by way of their preferred medium of communication and conveys that the Black male educator has listened, really listened, to the wishes of the caregiver. For many families, navigating the educational system can feel alienating or daunting. Black male educators who actively listen and validate caregivers' experiences build trust and lay the foundation for more meaningful collaborations, while also dispelling myths about Black males in the process.

Thriving as a with school relationships requires a multifaceted approach that blends resilience, cultural understanding, strategic advocacy, and strong communication skills. Whether building relationships with school administration, addressing sensitive issues like sexual harassment, navigating workplace gossip, or collaborating with caregivers, Black male educators have the opportunity to not only succeed in their careers but also drive meaningful change in their schools and communities. By remaining committed to professionalism, fostering respect, and building strong relationships, Black male educators are positioned to thrive and become transformative agents within the educational system.

To Thrive, Black male educators should:

1. Openly and regularly communicate with the school site administration
2. Seek out policies and reporting procedures regarding sexual harassment
3. Utilize approaches for addressing gossip
4. Provide Information, Workshops, and Support Groups

Questions for Reflection

1. What are some common misconceptions or biases that administrators, parents, or colleagues may have about Black male educators, and how can our school make plans to address these issues in constructive ways?
2. How can schools foster an environment where Black male educators feel safe, respected, and empowered to be their authentic selves in their professional relationships with administrators, parents, and colleagues?
3. How can our school site support Black male educators to find common ground with colleagues from diverse backgrounds while maintaining their own cultural identity and sense of self?

References

Bristol, T. J., & Mentor, M. (2018). Policing and teaching: The positioning of Black male teachers as agents in the universal carceral apparatus. *Urban Review, 50,* 218–234.

Clavell, J. (Director). (1967). *To Sir, with Love* [Film]. Columbia Pictures.

Collins, P. H. (2004). *Black sexual politics: African Americans, gender, and the new racism.* Routledge.

Louque, A., & Latunde, Y. (2014). Cultural capital in the village. The role African American families play in the education of children. *Multicultural Education,* 5–10.

Sandles, D. (2018). Black teachers: Surrogate parents and disciplinarians. *Journal for Leadership, Equity, and Research, 4*(1).

Sleeter, C. E. (2011). *The academic and social value of ethnic studies: A research review.* National Education Association.

Villegas, A. M., & Lucas, T. F. (2004). Diversifying the teacher workforce: A retrospective and prospective analysis. *Teachers College Record, 106*(13), 70–104.

CHAPTER 4

THRIVING WITH RESPONSIVE CLASSROOM GOVERNANCE

Teacher preparation programs around the globe offer a class on Classroom Management that outwardly purports to shape candidates' ideas about effective classroom structures and practices. When thinking about the notion of classroom management as a general concept, I am discomfited by the usage of this term in connection with classrooms, as it often signals a particular, socially acceptable kind of classroom control. Fundamentally, management as a field of study has its roots in organizational theory and emphasizes efficiency, productivity, and compliance among its core principles (Pindur et al., 1995). Further, the origins of the word *management* can be traced to the Latin phrase *manu agere*, meaning "to lead by the hand," which later evolved into the Italian word *maneggiare*, meaning to handle or to manage.

A less academic and etymological analysis of the word management leads to the conclusion that it has some patently chauvinistic elements. With the initial syllable of the word management, we see that the word part *man* starts the word. The relevance of that syllable here is that the notion of classical management theory was created and developed by European men with men in mind, considering only male sensibilities and aptitudes. While the second syllable, *age*, could arguably refer to one's chronological stage, and although there is embedded age discrimination in employment practices in various industries, there is little literature-based evidence to suggest the syllable has chronological age as its origin. With these two word parts, one could conclude that management as a practice was meant to oversee only men. Still, the general term management has other inherent associations that render it problematic. Terms such as *control, discipline,* and *punish* are regularly affixed to management, especially in classroom settings. And, for reasons such as the above, I elect to dispense with the term *classroom management* in favor of classroom governance, a shared governance at that. More to come on classroom governance.

As educators all over the world know, classroom expectations are typically designed to maintain order, establish boundaries, and create a positive learning environment. These expectations often focus on framing, some say controlling, student behavior, such as speaking respectfully, staying seated, following directions, and adhering to school-wide policies. However, many traditional classroom management systems adopt a one-size-fits-all approach that overlooks the cultural differences among students, particularly in diverse classrooms or those with students from marginalized communities. This lack of flexibility can lead to situations where students who don't conform to traditional norms are more likely to be reprimanded, punished, or misunderstood.

For many Black male educators, the problem with these traditional rules lies in how they intersect with perceptions of authority. Black male teachers are often subjected to biases and stereotypes that label them as overly authoritative, intimidating, or disciplinary. For Black male educators, if they adhere to the conventional notions of discipline, they tend to flourish; however, when classroom rules are enforced without consideration for students' cultural backgrounds or lived experiences, it can unintentionally alienate students and make it more difficult to build mutual respect. As outlined in Chapter 2, stereotypes about Black male educators abound and delimit the ideas in which they can operate. In many spaces, when Black male educators step outside those defined management parameters, they run afoul of school personnel. According to some, Black male teachers are veritable correctional officers in school settings that are extensions of prisons. Brown (2012) theorized that Black male teachers are a *pedagogical kind*, meaning they are the construct of many years of mounting conceptions about Black men in general.

Anecdote: *I remember one day early in my teaching career when a group of students decided to test me. I was a young Black male teacher at a mostly white school, and I could feel the weight of that dynamic. The class was rowdy, with students talking over me, ignoring instructions, and generally not listening. It was clear they were trying to see how much they could get away with. I could feel my patience slipping, but instead of raising my voice, I took a deep breath and said, "This is my classroom, but it's also* *yours. We can't do this without respect. If I let you talk over me, we're not learning anything."*

There was a long pause. Slowly, the room settled. I could see the shift in their faces; some realized I wasn't just here to go through the motions. By the end of the period, a couple of the most disruptive students apologized, acknowledging the respect we'd built together. It wasn't just about enforcing rules; it was about showing them I believed in them, and that I wasn't going to back down. I realized that classroom management, especially as a Black male teacher, was about more than just control, it was about building trust and holding space for respect on both sides.

Having a cohesive classroom environment also means that Black male educators cannot succumb to traditional patterns of classroom discipline. While the research on this subject is widespread and well-known, it certainly bears repeating that Black children are disproportionately expelled and suspended from school relative to their population. Sandles (2018) reported that Black children were nearly four times more likely to be suspended than white youth. Equally alarming is that six percent of all K-12 students were suspended from school at least once. At the heart of this exclusionary discipline is an adherence to age-old practices and ideologies that support removing students from the classroom when unwanted behavior arises. And, a major culprit in this brand of discipline is zero-tolerance policies that criminalize certain behaviors and unevenly penalize male students. Zero tolerance policies not only lead to student suspensions and expulsions, increasing dropout rates, but they can also introduce students to the juvenile justice system for the first time. A U.S. Department of Education study found that more than 70% of students arrested in school-related incidents or referred to law enforcement are Black students.

Copious research students have found that Black boys are often harshly punished and removed from the classroom when they violate school rules, while white students who commit the same infractions are excused, dismissed as simply being immature or acting like children. This differential treatment reveals a troubling double standard, where Black children are not only seen as more adult-like in their actions but are also frequently portrayed as beyond redemption. Society views Black people, across all ages, as perpetually guilty, making Black innocence seem like an unattainable ideal. This structural injustice perpetuates the false notion that Black individuals are incapable of growth or reform.

Classroom practices that exacerbate disproportionate punishments are probably too numerous to name, but Black male educators must be critical of every possible contribution to these injurious practices. Yelling at students, for example, is a practice that erodes students' self-concept and self-confidence. Further, this practice spirit murders children. According to Love (2016), "Spirit murdering within a school context is the denial of inclusion, protection, safety, nurturance, and acceptance because of fixed, yet fluid and moldable, structures of racism" (p. 2). Yet, this is common when teachers become frustrated with student misbehavior. Engaging in power struggles with students is another perilous venture that minimizes the respect factor of educators. Relatedly, Marzano and Marzano (2003) found that "Teachers who are overly focused on exerting authority may inadvertently provoke power struggles, hindering the development of trust and mutual respect in the classroom" (p. 13). These practices often contribute to a negative cycle, as students may internalize the frustration and respond with more disruptive behaviors, further reinforcing the stereotype of the *troublesome* student. Research has shown that when students are subjected to high levels of emotional distress or punitive actions, they are more likely to disengage from school, which in turn can negatively affect their academic performance and increase the likelihood of suspension.

Because learning institutions have been historically unkind to Black children, Black male educators must refrain from interactions that further develop distrust between the students and their families. The history of discriminatory practices in schools, including harsh disciplinary measures, has disproportionately impacted Black students, often leading to a pattern of over-policing and under-supporting these students. Disproportionate suspension rates for Black students, especially Black boys, highlight a broader issue of systemic inequities within the educational system. To address these disparities, Black male educators must not only provide a model of academic and behavioral excellence but also engage in practices that foster trust, open communication, and emotional support. Research by scholars such as Gloria Ladson-Billings emphasizes the importance of culturally responsive teaching, which recognizes and celebrates students' cultural backgrounds and seeks to build relationships based on mutual respect rather than authority.

> **Anecdote**: *When I started teaching, I wanted to be seen as firm. I had heard that I should not let students see me smile for the first few months and that I needed to show them who's boss. I didn't necessarily believe in that philosophy, but that is the way I was educated. In my third year of teaching, I was sitting in the cafeteria during parent conferences and overheard one of my former students (Antrelle) talking about me to a parent. 'You don't want your daughter in his class cuz he don't play.' I knew this was code for the teacher being mean, but I just knew he couldn't really feel that way about me. The following day I needed to get some clarification, so I went to Antrelle and told him I overheard the discussion and wanted to get some more understanding. Antrelle told me I was mean. 'Straight up, Mr. G. I won't even lie, you seem like you was always upset, and you didn't really listen to us. You're all about the rules, and it feels like you don't care about what we have to say.' I was taken aback. As a Black male teacher, I had prided myself on being firm, but hearing that I came across as uncaring was a punch to the gut. It made me rethink how I was approaching my role. I realized that being firm didn't mean being distant, and my students needed more than just structure; they*

needed empathy. From that moment on, I made a conscious effort to be more approachable, to listen more, and to find a balance between authority and compassion.

Through conventional classroom management practices, Black male educators can inadvertently contribute to the school-to-prison pipeline, which highlights the disturbing reality that punitive school practices disproportionately channel students, especially those of color, into the criminal justice system. Traditional methods, such as harsh disciplinary measures, suspensions, and expulsions, often reinforce the negative stereotypes about students of color, escalating minor infractions into major consequences. As a result, these students may face increased interaction with law enforcement, which can have long-term effects on their futures. Additionally, Black male educators, like all teachers, may unknowingly perpetuate these practices due to a lack of culturally responsive training or an overreliance on outdated disciplinary approaches.

Learning to Thrive

For Black male educators, the need for culturally responsive teaching practices is paramount in ensuring that all students feel valued, respected, and engaged. Classroom management is often seen as one of the most challenging aspects of teaching. However, traditional, one-size-fits-all methods of discipline may not be effective for every student, particularly in diverse classrooms. Culturally responsive classroom management takes into account the unique cultural backgrounds, identities, and experiences of students, allowing teachers to craft strategies that honor and respect these differences while maintaining a productive, respectful environment.

To be impactful leaders in the classroom, Black men must reject conventional conceptions of classroom management, which often problematize Black children and see them as behavioral challenges, and create a more connected, relational scheme for governing classrooms. In effect, Black male educators will thrive by establishing authority without relying on traditional discipline methods. To foster this brand of authority, Black males must present themselves as fair, decent, and honest. To be clear, this is a common expectation for educators, but it is especially important for Black male educators, who are unfairly saddled with increased expectations and are often unduly criticized. Fairness results from modeling oneself as objective and clear. Decency is the result of how Black educators treat colleagues, parents, and students, and honesty is demonstrated by doing what one says they are going to do and by being appropriately truthful. All of these attributes can be neatly codified through the artful crafting of classroom expectations.

Foundational to every effective classroom governance dynamic is a strong teacher-student connection. Historically, this is something that Black male educators have done very well. Creating a connection with students is natural to many Black men, who must learn to adapt to the various cultures of other people and therefore gain facility with so doing. Within institutions, however, educators are encouraged to get to know students in somewhat mechanical ways, such as using interest inventories and having students bring in a family artifact. While these techniques are portals to knowing about students, they cannot be the extent of the effort. Learning to thrive means Black male teachers must use the sometimes natural inclination to engage with different people to stimulate true rapport, more than just learning a student's name or their hobbies. This effort involves penetration of a student's psyche and an intimate understanding of a student's home context. Creating connections also involves a scientific approach to observation.

As mentioned in Chapter 2, classroom rules are often draconian and overwhelmingly favor the educator, regularly identifying *only* how the students should conduct themselves. To promote fairness, Black male educators should be willing to subject themselves to scrutiny from their students. The classroom expectations should be jointly constructed between students and the teacher and should specify how the Black male educator should treat students. This is a key element of *Responsive Classroom Governance* (RCG). Under this model, Black male teachers actively and intentionally work to reverse the trends that underserve Black and Brown students. The following techniques are recommended to develop RCG. Further, the RCG Framework creates an environment in which students take an active role in their education, relationships, and behavior by involving students in decision-making, teaching responsibility and accountability, fostering inclusivity, and emphasizing collaboration.

Co-create Classroom Expectations

In times past, teachers would often come on the first day of school and present a prefabricated list of rules that represented how students were supposed to behave. This list would be placed somewhere on the classroom walls and would usually be referenced when a student violated one of the rules. A common refrain might be, "Johnny, what is rule number 1?!" A significant challenge with that model is that teachers have biases and often very middle-class views, and when those are superimposed on students, an immediate chasm is formed. Using classroom rules in this traditional manner very much means that the teacher *rules* the classroom and uses the violation of classroom *rules* to discipline students. A problematic circumstance.

Instead, Black male educators should co-construct classroom expectations with their students. This process should include discussions around respect, kindness, collaboration, and responsibility. Students should feel that their voices matter in shaping how the classroom functions. To encourage participation in the process, educators should not start this process on the first day of school, as the initial meeting with students should be spent getting to know them, fostering comfort, and sharing with them what they will learn during the academic year. This works well for middle and high school classrooms. For elementary classroom spaces, a different approach would be in order, and the getting-to-know-you process should take place over the first half of the day, and the classroom expectations should be jointly crafted later in the day. The rationale behind delaying the classroom expectation work is that students are often reluctant to speak during the initial meeting. The first day of school is often fraught with anxiety and uncertainty, so time spent alleviating those feelings before encouraging students to vocally participate in the construction of classroom expectations is advisable.

To begin the work of co-constructing classroom expectations, it is vital to have students reflect on the questions to be discussed. In elementary classrooms, Black teachers might frontload students with the questions early in the day before engaging students in earnest discussion. For middle school and above, the teacher might review the questions or distribute them for students to ponder overnight. The following is a set of questions that can guide the construction of classroom expectations:

- What are some respectful ways to handle disagreements or disrespect in the classroom?
- What are the different ways students can share their ideas or concerns with the teacher?
- How can your teacher encourage you when you feel bad?
- What are some ways we can support students who speak different languages or dialects to feel comfortable in class?
- How can you show your teacher(s) that you appreciate them?
- How can your teacher(s) show their appreciation to you?

Once all the expectations are listed, the teacher and students should review them to ensure that everyone is on board. This can be done by asking each student to confirm if they agree with the statements. The teacher should also explain that this contract is a shared commitment to building a positive classroom community and remind students that this contract is a living document and can be revisited if needed. To demonstrate agreement, the teacher and students sign as a symbolic gesture of commitment to these shared values. This could be done digitally or on a printed document. The agreement should be posted somewhere visible in the classroom, like a bulletin board, as a constant reminder of the agreed-upon behaviors and expectations.

It is profoundly important that the Black male educator review aspects of the agreement daily and also as needed. For example, to begin the day, the teacher may say, "Yesterday we did an excellent job of supporting our classmates with language development, which is expectation number 4. Let's continue to improve at that, and remember to encourage students when they are struggling." In this way, the students get the needed reinforcement to continue the favorable behavior and they have regular contact with the classroom expectations. By making daily references to the expectations, the teacher ensures that students have consistent reminders, reinforcing a culture of accountability and shared responsibility.

Infusion of Music

RCG also thoughtfully incorporates music to help foster connections between students and teachers, especially when considering the unique role Black teachers play in the classroom. Music, particularly genres like rap and R&B, is a powerful tool for building bridges and creating a space of comfort and inclusivity for students. Black educators have long recognized the significance of music in connecting with their students, especially when it reflects their lived experiences and cultural background. By integrating music into classroom routines, teachers can set the tone for the day, signal transitions, and create an environment where students feel seen, supported, and understood. For example, playing an uplifting R&B song at the start of the day or a popular rap song during a break not only energizes the class but also invites students to express their identity through music that resonates with them.

In addition to influencing the classroom atmosphere, music helps create a sense of shared experience among students, especially when it includes genres they recognize and relate to. Teachers, particularly Black male educators, have used rap and R&B as tools to engage students, create a connection, and introduce culturally relevant lessons. These genres allow for rich discussions about culture, identity, and self-expression. Black male educators, such as those in urban schools, often turn to these genres as a way to communicate with their students in a language that feels familiar, fostering trust and understanding (Ladson-Billings, 1994). For instance, educators might use lyrics from a song by artists like Tupac Shakur or Aretha Franklin to illustrate concepts such as resilience, empowerment, or social justice, which can deepen students' understanding of academic material while simultaneously addressing their emotional and social needs. Research has shown that when students hear music they recognize, it helps them feel more comfortable and engaged in the learning process. Rap and R&B music, in particular, often highlight themes of community, struggle, and triumph, allowing students to connect with these themes on a personal level. For example, songs like Lauryn Hill's *Doo Wop* (That Thing) or Kendrick Lamar's *Alright* can provide a backdrop for discussions about self-respect, the importance of community, and social justice issues.

Music also teaches important lessons in self-regulation and responsibility. For students who may find it difficult to express their feelings, music provides an outlet for emotional release and reflection. Black teachers, particularly, understand the value of using music to help students process their emotions, whether they are feeling energized, anxious, or frustrated. When used mindfully, music helps signal transitions and set boundaries, teaching students when it is time to focus and when it is time to relax or celebrate (Kunjufu, 2005). This structure creates a classroom culture of respect and cooperation while ensuring that students feel heard and valued.

For example, teachers may use music to establish the tone for the lesson by saying, "Let's listen to a song to set the tone," and play a few minutes of a meaningful track. Once the song finishes, the teacher would seamlessly transition into the lesson, encouraging students to think about themes like respect or perseverance, using the lyrics as a starting point for discussion. Moreover, Black male teachers may center their music efforts on developing the social-emotional agency of their students. If students seem distracted or disengaged, the teacher might say, "Let's take a moment to reflect. I want you to listen to this song and think about what it means to you." After playing the song, the teacher might open up the floor for students to share their thoughts, helping them connect emotionally and refocus on the learning environment.

By incorporating music into the classroom, Black male educators create an environment where students feel recognized, particularly when the music aligns with their cultural identities and life experiences. This approach is particularly powerful for Black male teachers, who can use music as a tool to build trust, encourage engagement, and foster emotional development. Carefully selecting music, whether it's rap, R&B, or other genres, allows Black male educators to establish a classroom environment that encourages reflection and personal connection. Beyond enhancing academics, music provides a platform for students to express themselves, grow emotionally, and engage in important discussions around identity and community. Ultimately, weaving music into RCG creates a classroom culture of respect and collaboration, helping students thrive on both academic and emotional levels.

Move Moments

As a longtime teacher, I was fond of giving my students very brief learning breaks. I called them *move moments*. These were sometimes structured opportunities for students to momentarily escape from the cognitive demands we place on them. Sometimes, during a dense math period, I would say, "Okay, we need a move moment" and everyone would understand that this meant we would have some kind of physical activity for 2 minutes. Four corners, Simon Says, and silent ball are all chances for students to escape their challenging mental tasks by breaking up the effort. As importantly, Black educators must be intentional about having students move and be unapologetic in this approach, as there is a wealth of literature attesting to the idea that students, even older ones, require physical play. Not only are endorphins and receptivity to learning activated, but children are also more apt to freely laugh, talk, and share about themselves. This must be a purposeful move.

The study by Sibley and Etnier (2003) revealed a strong positive link between physical activity and cognitive functioning in children. While this information is not new or revelatory, it does beg the question of why more educators do not utilize physical activity as a strategy, particularly in communities with minority populations and lower education levels that generally have limited access to places for physical activity. For teachers and students to thrive, irrespective of grade level, there must be elements of physical activity incorporated throughout the instructional day. When I taught at the university level, I always sought to incorporate some kind of movement into class sessions as well. Take the following as a quantitative example. Depending on grade level, many K-12 students have approximately 360 instructional minutes per day. Deducting recess and/or lunchtime, elementary school students, for example, are in their seats for approximately 300 minutes per day, bereft of the chance to move and stimulate mental and physical growth. For Black male educators, intentionally incorporating physical movement into the classroom is about more than just giving students a break; it is a way to enhance both their cognitive and emotional development. These *move moments* can create opportunities to re-energize students and build stronger connections with them. When students take a quick moment to move, laugh, or engage in a light-hearted activity, they not only get a mental break but also feel more connected to their teacher, who is willing to recognize their need for balance. Black male teachers, in particular, have a unique opportunity to use these moments as a way to model care for their students, showing them that their mental, physical, and emotional well-being is important.

Additionally, physical activity serves as a powerful tool for building rapport. By integrating movement throughout the day, Black male educators can connect with students in informal ways that allow for personal moments of interaction outside the academic setting. These breaks provide insight into students' personalities and give teachers a chance to observe how they work with others or express themselves in a less structured environment. During these moments of movement, trust can be built, creating a foundation for deeper relationships. For Black male educators, this is not just about letting students stretch their legs, it is about creating a space where students feel valued, seen, and understood, ultimately helping them succeed in both their personal and academic journeys.

To conclude, RCG offers a powerful way for Black male educators to build a classroom environment rooted in fairness and mutual respect. By involving students in the creation of classroom expectations, teachers move beyond the traditional, top-down approach to discipline, encouraging a sense of shared responsibility and accountability. This approach is especially meaningful for Black and Brown students, who are often marginalized in more conventional classroom settings. Through RCG, Black male educators can foster stronger relationships with their students, promote inclusivity, and challenge the systems that have historically underserved them. Ultimately, RCG creates a classroom culture that supports both academic achievement and emotional well-being, allowing students to feel seen, heard, and empowered.

Conclusion

In navigating the intricate dynamics of classroom governance, Black male educators must challenge the traditional boundaries of classroom management and adopt practices that cultivate both academic excellence and emotional well-being. The history of systemic inequities in education, including the disproportionate punishment of Black students, reveals a pressing need for educators, particularly Black male teachers, to move beyond the limitations of conventional discipline. The shift toward a more responsive, culturally aware approach to governance is not simply a theoretical ideal but a practical necessity to address the deeply embedded disparities within the school system.

It is vital to recognize that the traditional model of classroom management, often steeped in ideas of control and compliance, overlooks the diversity of student experiences and backgrounds. As studies have shown, rigid disciplinary measures that fail to account for cultural differences can lead to alienation, punishment, and disengagement, further entrenching inequities. For Black male educators, this approach can be particularly fraught, as they navigate not only the challenges of managing a classroom but also the weight of racial stereotypes that can shape perceptions of their authority. These stereotypes often position Black male educators as figures of strict discipline, reinforcing societal biases about Black masculinity. However, when Black male teachers approach governance as an opportunity to build authentic relationships, to engage with students' lived experiences, and to honor their cultural backgrounds, they can shift the focus from authority to collaboration and mutual respect.

Ultimately, classroom governance must be redefined as a space for growth, not just for students, but for educators as well. By embracing a model of governance that prioritizes mutual respect and cultural awareness, Black male teachers can not only support their students' academic and social-emotional development but also contribute to a larger cultural shift within education—one that moves away from punitive measures and toward a more inclusive, compassionate approach. This transformation requires courage and a willingness to challenge deeply ingrained norms, but it is a necessary step in building classrooms where all students, especially those from historically marginalized communities, can thrive. In doing so, Black male educators will play a pivotal role in reshaping the future of education, fostering environments where all students are not only taught but truly seen and heard.

To Thrive, Black male educators should:

1. Co-Create classroom expectations
2. Infuse music into the classroom
3. Incorporate move moments

Questions for Reflection

1. In what ways does traditional classroom management theory overlook the cultural differences of students, particularly those from marginalized communities, and how can you adapt classroom expectations to be more inclusive?
2. How might your classroom management approach change if you focus more on building relationships and trust with students rather than adhering strictly to traditional disciplinary measures?
3. What is your understanding of the term "classroom management," and how does it align or conflict with the ideas of authority, respect, and cultural sensitivity in education?

References

Brown, A. L. (2012). On human kinds and role models: A critical discussion about the African American male teacher. *Educational Studies, 48*(3), 296–315.

Kunjufu, J. (2005). *Education of Black boys*. African American Images.

Ladson-Billings, G. (1994). What we can learn from multicultural education research. *Educational Leadership, 51*(8), 22–26.

Love, B. L. (2016). Anti-Black state violence, classroom edition: The spirit murdering of Black children. *Journal of Curriculum and Pedagogy, 13*(1), 22–25.

Marzano, R. J., & Marzano, J. S. (2003). The key to classroom management. *Educational Leadership, 61*(1), 6–13.

Pindur, W., Rogers, S. E., & Suk Kim, P. (1995). The history of management: A global perspective. *Journal of Management History, 1*(1), 59–77.

Sandles, D. (2018). Black teachers: Surrogate parents and disciplinarians. *Journal for Leadership, Equity, and Research, 4*(1).

Sibley, B. A., & Etnier, J. L. (2003). The relationship between physical activity and cognition in children: A meta-analysis. *Pediatric Exercise Science, 15*(3), 243–256.

CHAPTER 5

THE T'CHAKA EFFECT: BLACK MALE EDUCATOR MENTORSHIP

In the commercially successful and societally impactful movie *Black Panther*, the Wakandan king T'Challa receives timely and valuable support from his deceased father, T'Chaka. At critical stages during his development as king, T'Challa is guided by the spirit of T'Chaka and uses that wisdom to great effect. Sagacious words such as "A man who has not prepared his children for his own death has failed as a father" supply T'Challa with the paternal guidance and love he needs to effectively lead the African nation. As avowed *Black Panther* fans know very well, T'Challa eventually becomes a respected king, a renowned superhero, and a world leader.

Throughout the movie, numerous seminal moments supported T'Challa's growth and development and ushered him toward his route to the throne; however, always present, always influential were T'Chaka's resonant words and the memory of a father who had already served as the Wakandan king. "We are all one people. We are all connected in the great circle of life." Those and many other statements guided T'Challa and inspired the way he led the people. It is important to note that T'Chaka spoke with his father on the ancestral plane of existence, which is a spiritual realm where deceased Wakandans exist. A key bit of symbolism here is that ancestral guidance transcends physical life. T'Challa's connection to his father's wisdom highlights the deeply ingrained cultural belief in Wakanda that the wisdom of ancestors is not confined to the past but actively shapes and influences the present and future. In this realm, time and space blur, illustrating the continuous flow of generational knowledge.

Also symbolic from even a casual viewing of the movie is that director Ryan Coogler compellingly captured the essence of African communalism and deftly portrayed the essential theme of mentorship. To be clear, T'Challa had many mentors, including his magnificent queen mother, Ramonda, his sister, Shuri, the Council of Elders, and his trusted warriors, the Dora Milaje. Each invested in T'Challa and provided insight into what was an uncharted path for the forthcoming king. That said, the particular guidance of T'Chaka allowed T'Challa to develop into a viable leader, and it was only T'Chaka who could advise T'Challa about the vagaries of serving the people as their king.

T'Chaka's impact was not unlike that of Black male educators who support, guide, and lead other Black male educators during the often labyrinthine path of becoming an educator and also once they enter the field. The T'Chaka effect is something that every Black male educator needs, and as much as mentorship can and does come from various quarters, the potency of one Black male educator mentoring another cannot be encapsulated within words. The shared lived experiences, mutual understanding, and common struggles make the connection between mentor and mentee unique and deeply transformative. Like T'Chaka's leadership in *Black Panther*, these mentors provide more than just guidance. They instill a sense of community, professional development, robust emotional support, and girding to confront anti-Blackness. The T'Chaka effect goes beyond advice; it is about empowering Black male educators to persevere, find their voice, and embrace their purpose in the classroom, ensuring they thrive in an often challenging and isolating profession.

Mentoring Black Male Teachers

Black male teachers in the US are often tasked with the dual role of providing mentorship to Black male students and serving as mentors to other Black male teachers. However, despite the recognition of the importance of Black male educators in fostering the academic success and emotional well-being of Black male students, Black male teachers remain significantly underrepresented in the educational system. This shortage is particularly concerning, as Black male teachers are often recruited with the assumption that they can effectively serve as mentors for Black male students, a notion supported by some research (Scott et al., 2013). Yet, this assumption, while valuable, can sometimes overshadow the pedagogical strengths that Black male educators bring to the classroom. Black male teachers, when provided with culturally relevant curriculum and professional support, can craft instruction that connects deeply with students' lived experiences and cultural identities, which is a stronger, more pedagogically grounded argument for recruiting and retaining them (Pabon et al., 2011; Lynn, 2006). Put differently, Black men intuitively know how to engage with and support other Black men educators, as they have experienced many of the same triumphs, challenges, and daily demands.

Mentorship among Black male educators goes beyond just guiding students; it is also crucial for nurturing the professional growth of fellow educators. Research highlights how mentorship between Black male teachers creates a unique bond based on shared cultural experiences and understanding of systemic challenges within education. By supporting each other through the shared struggles of underrepresentation, racial biases, and the stress of teaching in predominantly white institutions, Black male teachers can create a supportive network that fosters professional development and emotional resilience (Lindwall, 2017). This mentorship dynamic is not just about professional advice or classroom management; it also emphasizes the importance of self-care, emotional intelligence, and personal growth, empowering Black male teachers to navigate their careers with confidence.

> **Anecdote**: *I would not have made it without my two mentors. One of them was a VP at the middle school, but he made time for me at least once per week, and he always let me call or text when I had a situation at work. The other one was a teacher at my school site. He had been around for about 20 years by that time, and he always had the coolest demeanor. Nothing seemed to bother him, although I think he was probably just over a lot of the things that happened at school. Both of them just would not let me quit. They knew each other and probably talked about me sometimes, but they would be delivering the same messages and those words were always exactly what I needed to hear. Now, 15 years into the profession, I try to reach out to young brothas and sisters whenever I see them around. Some of them don't listen, but I'm still gonna reach out to them.*

As such, Black male teachers mentoring other Black male teachers is an essential practice in both supporting new educators and creating a lasting legacy of leadership in the field. By fostering a strong network of mentorship, Black male teachers can ensure that the next generation of educators is not only prepared to excel in the classroom but also equipped to address the challenges of the educational system, push for systemic reforms, and advocate for the needs of their students. This process ultimately reinforces the broader goals of Black educators in shaping equitable and culturally relevant educational environments for all students, but particularly those who are often marginalized in traditional school settings.

Mentoring Black Male Students

While it is not the chief focus of this piece, the role Black male educators play in mentoring students is also vital, as Black students in US public schools face significant challenges, which underscores the importance of Black male teachers in supporting their success. Importantly, emerging research provides insight into the positioning of Black male educators in terms of student achievement. Research indicates that Black male teachers are more inclined to adopt culturally responsive teaching methods, which resonate with their students' experiences and identities. Furthermore, Black male teachers are uniquely positioned to guide students through issues of racial identity and discrimination, helping students through the complexities of navigating racism both within the school environment and beyond. Through these intentional efforts, they help foster resilience and empowerment among their students.

Further, Black male mentorship of students brings a powerful and valuable perspective to teaching that helps mentees navigate the complexities of diverse classrooms and workplaces. Like T'Challa, mentees who follow the guidance of their mentors tend to thrive and can better understand the path forward to successfully navigate personal workplace challenges, difficulties with planning, and communication with site administrators. Often, when circumstances like school site squabbles surface, the mentees have a growth opportunity to learn best practices in dealing with them and understand appropriate techniques for addressing the associated social-emotional problems. Black male educator guidance is especially significant for preservice teachers, particularly those working in schools with a high percentage of students from various cultural and socioeconomic backgrounds. Importantly, Black male teachers, drawing from their own lived experiences and cultural insights, are uniquely qualified to mentor others in implementing these practices.

The Ancestral Plane

The guidance Black male mentors provide to mentees has uncommon and enduring power. This is axiomatic but requires a statement. In *Black Panther*, T'Challa drew great strength and guidance from his conversations with T'Chaka in the ancestral plane. These discussions allowed T'Challa to challenge his father, reflect on the exchanges, and create new understandings about his personal growth, which led to expanded leadership agency. Similarly, Black male teacher mentors foster the same kind of growth opportunities, exhorting their Black male mentees to construct their own reality of teaching under the guidance and tutelage of an experienced leader.

The value of Black male educators being mentored is immense, as it not only enhances their professional growth but also provides a critical support system for navigating the unique challenges they face in educational spaces. What is clear from the literature on Black male teachers is that they often occupy a space that is both powerful and precarious, particularly in environments where they are underrepresented or isolated, and mentorship becomes an essential tool for sustaining them in these roles, providing guidance, encouragement, and strategies to overcome obstacles they may encounter in their careers. This mentorship is not just about classroom management or instructional techniques; it's about fostering a sense of belonging, cultivating resilience, and helping these educators realize their full potential as both educators and leaders.

It is also clear that Black male educators face distinct challenges, including the weight of cultural expectations, racial biases, and a lack of professional support within predominantly white educational institutions. For many, the experience of being one of the few Black male teachers in their schools can be isolating, as they navigate microaggressions, implicit biases, and sometimes even outright discrimination. Mentorship offers a safe space for these educators to process these experiences, gain perspective, and build the emotional intelligence needed to respond to such challenges effectively. In this regard, Black male mentors serve as a lifeline, providing not only professional advice but also emotional and psychological support that helps them maintain their sense of identity, purpose, and self-worth.

The mentorship of Black male educators also allows them to develop a more expansive view of their role in the classroom. Too often, Black male teachers are seen only as disciplinarians or role models, with their broader contributions to education undervalued or overlooked. A teacher mentor can help them see beyond these limitations, encouraging them to embrace their leadership potential in other aspects of the educational experience. Through mentorship, Black male educators learn to see themselves as advocates for social change, stewards of a culturally relevant pedagogy, and architects of educational spaces that nurture and empower their students. These mentors help them understand that their work is not just about teaching content; it's about shaping minds, challenging systems, and creating spaces for Black excellence to flourish.

Additionally, mentoring helps Black male educators build a sense of solidarity and collective purpose within the profession. By learning from others who share their background, experiences, and vision for education, these educators begin to understand that their struggles are not isolated; they are part of a broader movement to transform the educational landscape for Black students and educators alike. This sense of community reinforces their commitment to their work and provides a network of support that extends beyond their own classrooms, encouraging them to persevere through difficult times and to remain dedicated to their mission. When Black male educators mentor each other, they create a lasting legacy that builds the foundation for future generations of Black teachers who can continue the cycle of growth, advocacy, and empowerment.

In a more practical sense, mentorship also offers Black male educators the opportunity to learn effective strategies for navigating the institutional complexities of the educational system. Whether it's understanding how to advocate for resources, manage professional development, or approach difficult conversations with colleagues and administrators, mentorship equips them with the tools to succeed in a system that is often stacked against them. Through these relationships, they gain access to knowledge and networks that can help propel their careers forward, opening doors to leadership positions, policy influence, and broader educational reform efforts.

Building Community and Networks

One of the most vital aspects of mentorship for Black male educators is the establishment of a strong community and network of support, much like the vital network of support that T'Challa receives throughout *Black Panther*. As T'Challa leans on the counsel of his father, T'Chaka, and other key figures like his sister Shuri and the Dora Milaje, Black male educators benefit from similar support systems within their professional journeys. These mentors form a community where shared experiences and cultural understandings foster unity and belonging, providing Black male educators with not only practical advice but also emotional support and solidarity. Much like the interconnectedness T'Challa experiences in the *Black Panther* narrative, these networks create an enduring bond that helps combat the isolation that many Black male educators face in predominantly white institutions. The value of community is not just about surviving in isolation but thriving in unity, strengthening these educators' sense of identity within the profession (Garcia & Tyler, 2019).

Moreover, the sense of community and network-building established through mentorship mirrors the collective strength of Wakanda in *Black Panther*, where the people are united by a common cause and a shared understanding of their culture. This collaborative spirit allows mentors and mentees to exchange strategies, resources, and experiences that help both parties navigate their challenges and celebrate victories. The collective network that emerges not only supports Black male educators but also ensures that their struggles are recognized and addressed, just as T'Challa's growth as a leader is supported by his community of mentors (Garcia & Tyler, 2019).

Anecdote: *People say you have to find your tribe, and that's especially true in teaching. Over the past seven years, I've taught at two different schools, and at both of them, I was the only Black person on staff. At first, it was isolating. I quickly realized that while I was part of a team of educators, I needed a space where I could be fully myself, understood, and supported. That's when I met Mr. Michael, another teacher at a different school. We clicked right away, even though we teach different grades. We quickly became more intentional about supporting each other. We created our own network, a space to talk about the stressors we faced and celebrate the small wins that often go unnoticed. Now, we've built a solid support system. Sometimes, Mr. Michael sends me inspirational quotes during lunch, reminding me why I do this work. In return, I'll send him funny videos throughout the day to lighten the mood. Those small gestures help remind me that I'm not alone. It's those moments of connection that make all the difference, especially on the toughest days. Finding my tribe, like Mr. Michael, has been a game-changer in keeping me resilient and motivated to keep going.*

Additionally, mentorship plays an essential role in the professional development of Black male educators, providing them with the tools and insights necessary to succeed in their careers, much like the mentorship that T'Challa receives throughout *Black Panther*. Just as T'Challa's growth as a leader is shaped by the wisdom of his father, T'Chaka, Black male educators draw on the experiences of their mentors to navigate the challenges of classroom management, curriculum design, and the complexities of school culture. Mentors, much like the guidance T'Challa receives from his father on the ancestral plane, offer invaluable, lived advice. They share their own journeys to help mentees develop effective teaching strategies and better understand the diverse needs of their students. This guidance refines teaching methods, ultimately improving student outcomes, much like T'Challa's evolving leadership skills, honed through the support of his mentors.

Professional Development

In *Black Panther*, T'Challa's journey is not just about inheriting the throne; it is about evolving as a leader who possesses wisdom, emotional intelligence, and the ability to adapt to unforeseen challenges. Throughout the film, T'Challa grapples with the complexities of leadership, especially when faced with crises like the arrival of Erik Killmonger, who challenges Wakanda's policies and principles. T'Challa's leadership grows as he learns to embrace the lessons from his father, T'Chaka, and the guidance of others, allowing him to transcend traditional views of kingship. His leadership becomes rooted in a deep understanding of community, responsibility, and long-term vision, demonstrating the value of mentorship that teaches not only the technical aspects of leadership but also the deeper, philosophical elements of guiding a nation through difficult times. Similarly, Black male mentors help educators navigate the bureaucratic complexities and challenges of the educational system, which can often feel as daunting as the political struggles T'Challa faces. Whether it's advocating for necessary resources, seeking out professional development, or engaging in meaningful dialogue with administrators, mentors provide strategic, nuanced advice to help mentees succeed in environments that can sometimes feel stifling or unsupportive.

Much like T'Challa's evolution from a reluctant ruler to a wise king, Black male educators, under the guidance of their mentors, are encouraged to expand their leadership beyond traditional roles within the classroom. These mentors, through shared lived experiences, equip their mentees with the confidence and understanding necessary to take on leadership roles that influence the broader educational landscape. T'Challa's leadership was transformative not just for Wakanda but for the global stage, as he recognized the need for broader change and reform in the world. Similarly, Black male educators are empowered to take part in educational reforms that challenge systemic issues and advocate for policies that support equity, inclusion, and representation. The mentorship they receive is foundational not only for their immediate growth but also for sustainable progress within the field of education. Just as T'Challa's guidance transforms him into a leader capable of shaping the future of Wakanda, Black male educators' development through mentorship opens doors to leadership and policy-making roles that extend far beyond the classroom, ultimately contributing to long-lasting change in the educational system. This journey, like T'Challa's, is about more than individual success; it is about shaping the future for others, particularly those who have been historically marginalized (Morrison & Hauser, 2020).

Emotional Support

The emotional and psychological challenges that Black male educators face are often overlooked, yet mentorship plays a critical role in providing the support necessary to navigate these hurdles. Just as T'Challa receives crucial emotional guidance from his father, T'Chaka, in *Black Panther*, Black male educators often find themselves confronting not only professional challenges but also the emotional tolls of systemic racial biases. In the film, T'Challa struggles with the weight of leadership, the loss of his father, and his self-doubt about his ability to lead Wakanda. He is emotionally tested at multiple points, but his father's spirit, especially in moments of crisis, offers T'Challa the wisdom to reflect and move forward with a greater sense of clarity and responsibility. Similarly, Black male educators often face a combination of systemic oppression, racial microaggressions, and implicit biases that takes an emotional toll. Mentorship helps these educators process their emotional struggles, offering them the opportunity to confront feelings of isolation, inadequacy, and frustration that arise in environments where they may be underrepresented. Like T'Challa, who finds solace and guidance from T'Chaka's words, Black male educators are provided with the emotional support they need to navigate the unique challenges they encounter, allowing them to strengthen their emotional resilience and maintain a clear sense of purpose.

In *Black Panther*, T'Challa's emotional growth is not only about overcoming his doubts but also about understanding the importance of emotional intelligence in leadership. He learns that being a good leader is not only about strategy or power but about understanding one's own feelings and being emotionally in tune with those one leads. This emotional evolution parallels the experiences of Black male educators, who, through mentorship, are encouraged to build their own emotional resilience and develop strategies for self-care. Just as T'Challa grows stronger through his reflections with T'Chaka, Black male educators are reminded by their mentors that caring for their emotional well-being is vital for their longevity in the profession. Mentors help them cultivate emotional intelligence, understanding their own emotions, managing stress, and using emotional experiences as a source of strength. This mentorship enables them not only to cope with daily challenges but to transform stress into productive action, advocating for students and pushing for changes that will improve the educational landscape for all. Mentorship fosters a supportive relationship in which these educators are reminded of their worth, reaffirming that they are not alone in their struggles. Just as T'Challa learns to embrace his full potential as a king and leader, Black male educators are empowered to thrive in a profession that can often be draining and emotionally taxing. Through mentorship, they develop the tools necessary to persist, not just for their own sake but for the future of the students they serve, ultimately ensuring that their emotional well-being is preserved as they continue to contribute meaningfully to the profession.

Learning to Thrive

Given the profound impact mentorship can have, establishing a structured and intentional framework to equip Black male educators with the tools and resources needed for success is crucial. Effective mentorship for Black male teachers should be both purposeful and holistic, combining professional development with emotional support to help them navigate the complexities and unique challenges of the educational landscape. This mentorship not only allows Black male educators to refine their teaching practices but also empowers them to develop strong leadership skills, confront racial challenges, and cultivate culturally responsive classrooms that reflect their students' diverse needs. By offering Black male educators a robust network of guidance and support, they are better positioned to thrive in their roles, build resilience, and realize their full potential as educators and leaders. The following techniques outline essential components of a mentorship framework that can enable Black male educators to excel, fostering both their personal and professional growth in a way that sets them up for long-term success.

Work-Life Balance and Well-Being

A structured mentorship program can offer Black male educators strategies for maintaining a healthy work-life balance in a profession known for its burnout rates. Given the emotional and mental toll teaching can take, especially in challenging environments, mentors can help mentees set boundaries, prioritize self-care, and manage their workload effectively. Encouraging time management and well-being practices ensures that Black male educators can continue to bring their best selves to the classroom while safeguarding their personal health. While a perfect work-life balance is difficult to establish, relative balance can be a more realistic goal, with specific emphasis on finding time each day to engage in at least one self-care activity.

Navigating Implicit Bias and Stereotyping

Black male educators often face stereotypes related to their race and gender. Mentors can help mentees understand and counteract implicit biases they may encounter, both from students and colleagues. This guidance can extend to helping mentees navigate professional situations where they may be unfairly labeled as *aggressive, angry,* or *overbearing,* ensuring they learn how to assert their authority while challenging these preconceived notions with confidence and professionalism. Specifically, mentorship should position Black males to address implicit bias and stereotypes in the workplace in a manner that is consistent with the organization's protocols. Therefore, mentors should equip mentees with the policies on filing complaints and learning the discrimination policies outlined in the school or district. Often, these can be found on the organization's website, but the mentor can provide concrete guidance on how those features really work, and the mentor can direct mentees to trusted individuals who might take complaints seriously.

Sustaining Passion and Purpose

Undoubtedly, mentors can play a crucial role in helping Black male educators sustain their passion for teaching by reminding them of the larger purpose behind their work. Whether it's advocating for student success, mentoring future generations, or making a difference in their community, mentorship helps reconnect educators with their core motivations. Mentors can provide the encouragement needed to persevere, especially in challenging times when they may feel isolated or unsupported. One way mentors can support mentees in this way by having them use a cueing device or system that is reminiscent of the purpose. As an example, a mentor may use painted rocks with quote listed. I have seen rocks that use "Be quick but don't hurry," and "Love what you do," etc. In other instances, educators strategically post pictures of their family or a small vision board that depicts their goals.

Navigating Career Pathways

One key aspect of mentorship is helping Black male educators identify opportunities for career advancement. For many Black male educators, the path to career growth may not always be immediately clear, and having a mentor who can offer guidance and direction is essential. This process involves more than just advice on climbing the professional ladder; it encompasses a comprehensive approach to recognizing and seizing opportunities that align with the educator's unique interests, strengths, and aspirations. Mentors can help their mentees explore various pathways, such as pursuing advanced degrees, earning certifications, or taking on leadership roles within their schools. For instance, a mentor might recommend pursuing graduate education in educational leadership or curriculum design, or they could guide a mentee toward administrative positions, such as assistant principal or principal, where they can have a larger impact on school culture and student outcomes.

In addition to educational advancement, mentors can also help Black male educators explore transitions into other areas within the education field. For example, many Black male educators may be interested in making the shift into counseling, where they can support students' social-emotional development, or policy-making, where they can influence broader educational reforms. By sharing insights into the diverse opportunities available in education, mentors help their mentees understand that career advancement is not limited to classroom teaching alone and that there are numerous avenues to influence education at the systemic level.

Mentorship also plays a crucial role in guiding the practical steps needed to achieve these career goals. Mentors can help Black male educators navigate the landscape of professional development programs, identifying those that will provide the most benefit to their careers. Whether it's enrolling in leadership training, joining professional associations, or pursuing workshops on effective teaching strategies, mentors can assist their mentees in finding the resources and networks that will elevate their professional skills. Furthermore, mentors can provide valuable advice on how to strategically network with other educators, administrators, and policymakers, fostering relationships that may open doors to new opportunities. They can also advise on how to cultivate a strong professional reputation, which is key for gaining visibility in leadership circles and for future career advancements.

Conclusion

In conclusion, mentorship is an indispensable tool for Black male educators, providing a pathway not only to professional growth but also to personal empowerment. A well-structured mentorship framework, grounded in both professional development and emotional support, is essential for helping Black male educators navigate the complexities of their careers while fostering resilience and leadership skills. By addressing key areas such as work-life balance, navigating implicit bias, sustaining passion and purpose, and advancing careers, mentors offer invaluable guidance that helps Black male educators thrive in their roles and contribute meaningfully to their communities.

As these educators gain the confidence to confront challenges and seize opportunities, mentorship becomes a transformative experience that encourages them to grow as individuals and leaders. Whether it's finding ways to prioritize self-care or exploring new career pathways, mentors provide the encouragement and tools necessary for Black male educators to succeed in a profession often fraught with unique obstacles. Through ongoing mentorship, Black male educators can not only overcome systemic barriers but also thrive in their careers, cultivating classrooms that reflect their values and fostering an environment of growth for their students.

Ultimately, mentorship is about more than just career advancement, it's about creating a support system that allows Black male educators to realize their full potential, sustain their passion for teaching, and continue making a profound impact on future generations. By investing in mentorship, we ensure that Black male educators are equipped to lead with confidence, integrity, and purpose, paving the way for long-lasting success in education and beyond. Just as T'Chaka did for T'Challa.

To Thrive, Black male educators should:

1. Develop Work-Life Balance and Well-Being
2. Navigate Implicit Bias and Stereotyping
3. Sustain Passion and Purpose
4. Navigate Career Pathways

Questions for Reflection

1. How can mentorship help Black male educators balance the emotional toll of teaching while maintaining their passion for the profession?
2. How can Black male educators use visual cues, such as a vision board or motivational quotes, to reconnect with their purpose in teaching?
3. What do you believe is the most important role of mentorship for Black male educators, and why?

References

Garcia, D. R., & Tyler, K. M. (2019). Building communities through mentorship: The role of African American male educators in supporting one another. *Journal of Education for Diversity, 25*(4), 12–24.

Lindwall, A. (2017). Mentorship of Black male teachers: Addressing racial barriers and cultivating cultural relevance. *Journal of Teacher Education, 68*(2), 141–158.

Lynn, M. (2006). Race, culture, and the socialization of Black male teachers. *Teaching and Teacher Education, 22*(3), 370–383.

Morrison, S. P., & Hauser, S. D. (2020). The critical role of mentorship in the professional development of Black male teachers. *International Journal of Teacher Education, 37*(2), 95–107.

Pabon, A. M., Anderson, G., & Kharem, H. (2011). Re-thinking the mentoring of Black male teachers: Toward a culturally relevant model. *Urban Education, 46*(6), 842–866.

Scott, J., Taylor, E., & Palmer, L. (2013). The role of mentorship in the professional development of Black male educators. *International Journal of Educational Leadership, 17*(4), 73–85.

CHAPTER 6

SEIZE THE TIME TO THRIVE: EMPOWERING BLACK MALE EDUCATORS AGAINST RACIAL MICROAGGRESSIONS

Teaching is an inherently demanding profession, but for Black male educators, the challenges are compounded by a constant barrage of psychological assaults, many of which remain invisible to those outside our lived experiences. While overt forms of racial discrimination, macroaggressions, are often more easily recognized and addressed, Black male educators frequently face microaggressions: subtle, yet deeply damaging acts of racial bias. These smaller, cumulative assaults, though often dismissed as insignificant by others, result in profound emotional and psychological strain that builds over time, shaping both our professional identity and personal well-being.

Growing up in Oakland, California, I was acutely aware of the presence and influence of the Black Panther Party for Self-Defense. However, it wasn't until later in life that I began to truly understand how the Party's principles of resistance, empowerment, and self-advocacy have shaped my own approach to life and teaching. I now realize how much their commitment to confronting systemic injustice and uplifting Black communities parallels the daily struggles Black educators regularly face in the classroom.

A Black Panther Party Overview

In 1966, in the heart of Oakland, two Black male college students, Huey P. Newton and Bobby Seale, decided to challenge the oppressive police practices that had long brutalized unarmed Black people in the streets. Their initial efforts led to the creation of the Black Panther Party, a revolutionary political organization that grew rapidly, with more than 60 chapters worldwide. Aligned with the Party's 10-point program, these chapters embodied a collective fight for justice and equality, principles that would inspire future generations, including myself. However, the Black Panther Party was not merely a protest movement; it was a call to action. It sought to dismantle systemic racism, promote self-defense, and advocate for social and economic equality. Through programs like free food distribution, health clinics, and Liberation Schools, the Party gave marginalized communities the resources and knowledge to empower themselves. One of the most impactful of these programs was the Free Breakfast for Children initiative, launched in 1969. The program was designed to address food insecurity, providing meals to children in underserved neighborhoods. Across cities like Oakland, Los Angeles, Chicago, and New York, it served thousands of children daily, giving them not only nourishment but also a sense of dignity and support.

The Black Panther Party's Legacy and Influence

The Black Panther Party's influence on me as a Black male educator is profound and enduring. In the face of microaggressions and systemic challenges, their legacy serves as a constant reminder of the importance of standing firm in my commitment to serve and uplift the next generation. Like the Party's initiatives, the role of an educator extends far beyond teaching academic content, it is about fostering a sense of empowerment, pride, and resilience within students. Just as the Panthers worked tirelessly to address the needs of their communities, Black male educators must also strive to equip students with the tools and encouragement necessary to confront the unique challenges they face, particularly those rooted in racial bias and inequality. The legacy of the Black Panther Party not only serves as a powerful model but also as a crucial reminder: the struggle for justice is ongoing, and we must persist in challenging the systems that perpetuate racial discrimination and inequity, both in and outside the classroom.

What Are Racial Microaggressions?

Microaggressions, a term coined by psychiatrist Franklin Pierce in 1973, are subtle, often unnoticed forms of racial bias that occur frequently in daily life and have significant, cumulative effects on the well-being of marginalized individuals. These behaviors, which can manifest in many forms, are particularly pervasive in educational settings and present significant challenges for Black male educators. Microaggressions are not isolated incidents; rather, they represent a broader pattern of racial discrimination that impacts Black male educators both personally and professionally. In the context of education, these microaggressions can take many forms, including subtle biases in interactions with colleagues, students, parents, and administrators. As Black male educators are already tasked with the emotional and physical labor of supporting underserved students, the added weight of these microaggressions only compounds their struggles, creating a hostile and often unwelcoming environment.

Microaggressions can be categorized into three distinct forms: microassaults, microinsults, and microinvalidations, each with its own unique effects. *Microassaults* are overt, intentional discriminatory actions, such as racial slurs or excluding someone based on their identity. These behaviors are easier to recognize but still contribute to a hostile environment, affecting both the emotional and professional experiences of Black male educators. *Microinsults* are more subtle and often unintentional, such as comments about someone's articulation or intelligence, which imply surprise or doubt based on their racial background. While these actions may seem harmless to the observer, their cumulative impact on Black male educators can significantly undermine their self-esteem and sense of belonging. Finally, *microinvalidations* occur when the experiences or feelings of marginalized individuals are dismissed or minimized. For instance, telling a Black educator that "race doesn't matter here" or "I don't see color" invalidates the unique struggles they face and erases their lived experiences. These microinvalidations can be particularly damaging because they deny the reality of systemic racism, further isolating Black male educators in their professional environments.

The persistent nature of these microaggressions contributes to the underrepresentation of Black male educators in the teaching profession. Despite their qualifications and capabilities, Black male educators often face subtle but significant barriers that prevent them from advancing, reinforcing systemic inequities that are difficult to address. As these microaggressions accumulate over time, they not only affect the effectiveness of Black male educators but also take a toll on their mental health and professional growth. By understanding the different types of microaggressions and their cumulative impact, we can begin to address the systemic issues that hinder the success and well-being of Black male educators in the classroom and beyond.

This chapter aims to unpack the impact of racial microaggressions on Black male educators, examining how these biases manifest in the classroom and beyond. By exploring their effects, we will discuss strategies for Black Panther-like resistance, institutional responses, and ways to cultivate more supportive environments for Black male teachers.

The Impact of Racial Microaggressions

Racial microaggressions profoundly impact both the professional identity and personal well-being of Black male educators. These acts of discrimination undermine their confidence, sense of competence, and emotional health. Over time, the cumulative impact of these microaggressions can cause lasting harm, affecting the educator's ability to succeed in their role and, in some cases, prompting them to reconsider their career in education. When microaggressions occur, such as being mistaken for staff members like security guards or disciplinarians rather than teachers, they subtly diminish their authority and credibility in the eyes of others. The ongoing scrutiny of their abilities, along with the constant need to prove themselves in ways their white colleagues do not, gradually diminishes their confidence. Over time, this can undermine their professional identity and teaching effectiveness.

Black male educators are often placed in the impossible position of balancing unrealistic and contradictory expectations, as they are expected to be role models for all students, especially Black students, yet simultaneously stereotyped as overly authoritative or less competent. Microaggressions that suggest they are *natural* disciplinarians or that comment on their *intimidating* presence reinforce these limiting stereotypes, stifling their ability to express themselves authentically. The emotional toll of managing these conflicting expectations can lead to burnout as Black male educators navigate overt and covert racial biases while striving to perform their professional duties.

The cumulative effect of these microaggressions creates a heavy emotional toll, as Black male educators are forced to prove their competence repeatedly in ways that their white colleagues do not. The constant pressure to demonstrate their worth and challenge biased perceptions of their abilities can contribute to stress, anxiety, and even burnout. These microaggressions, though subtle, create a work environment where Black male educators are not able to thrive to their full potential. The emotional and professional toll is significant and can lead to feelings of isolation, disillusionment, and fatigue, which affect their ability to remain engaged and passionate about their teaching (Sue et al., 2007). Furthermore, these microaggressions can make it more difficult for Black male educators to envision a successful and long-term career in the education system, especially when they are systematically excluded from leadership opportunities and support structures designed to foster professional growth.

The reach of these microaggressions extends beyond the workplace and deeply affects the personal well-being of Black male educators. The emotional and psychological toll of constant discrimination can result in feelings of frustration, anger, and exhaustion. As they face these challenges day after day, they may experience "racial battle fatigue," a form of chronic vigilance that fosters anxiety, depression, and stress (Smith et al., 2007).

This emotional burden can reduce their ability to engage effectively with students and colleagues, thereby diminishing their professional impact.

The added stress of microaggressions compounds the natural challenges of the teaching profession. Black male educators are not only responsible for managing classrooms, creating engaging lessons, and supporting students, but they also navigate the additional challenge of facing racial discrimination daily. The constant pressure to prove themselves, combined with the toll of working in a racially unwelcoming environment, can result in burnout (Berry, 2018). This perpetual strain leaves little space for self-care, ultimately leading to job dissatisfaction and physical health issues such as sleep disturbances and high blood pressure (refer to Chapter 1) (Williams, 1997).

In time, Black male educators may begin to internalize the harmful messages perpetuated by microaggressions. They may feel inferior, less competent, or disconnected from their professional identity (Clark et al., 1999). Internalizing stereotypes, such as the assumption that Black educators are less capable or that their authority is inherently questioned, can foster self-doubt and weaken their sense of purpose (Sue et al., 2007). This erodes their motivation and impacts their ability to stay connected to their students and the teaching profession.

Moreover, microaggressions can create a sense of isolation for Black male educators, particularly when they lack support from peers or administrators. These subtle acts of racial discrimination often go unacknowledged, leaving educators feeling alienated. In environments where such behavior is tolerated or ignored, Black male educators may feel they have no space to express their concerns, exacerbating their sense of isolation (Solórzano et al., 2000). This lack of support can have serious consequences on their mental health, leaving them emotionally drained and disconnected from their professional community (Sue et al., 2007).

Student Interactions and Racial Microaggressions

Black male educators face numerous racial microaggressions in their interactions with students, which can have a profound impact on both their professional identity and classroom dynamics. One of the most common stereotypes projected onto Black male educators is that they are inherently aggressive or domineering. This perception can lead students to misinterpret the educator's authority, viewing their teaching style as excessively strict or harsh when it may simply be a structured approach to classroom governance. As a result, students may respond to these educators with resistance, undermining their authority or dismissing their teaching methods based on preconceived notions rather than an objective evaluation of their skills and expertise.

The racial biases projected onto Black male educators are compounded by the unequal expectations that students place on them. For example, students may expect Black male educators to be natural disciplinarians and assume that their role is to enforce rules rather than foster student growth and academic development. This expectation can create additional pressure for Black male educators, who must constantly navigate the delicate balance between maintaining authority and being perceived as approachable or empathetic. The burden of meeting these exaggerated demands often leads to burnout and emotional exhaustion, as these educators are forced to engage in a perpetual balancing act where their authority is scrutinized more than that of their white counterparts (Solórzano, 2000).

Moreover, microaggressions from students further reinforce systemic biases in the classroom, contributing to a broader culture of racial inequity in education. These biases can manifest in various forms, such as students assuming that Black educators are less capable of nurturing academic talent or expecting them to fulfill stereotypical roles like those of a *cool* or *tough* teacher. This type of racialized thinking influences how students interact with their educators, undermining the professional rapport and mutual respect that are essential for fostering a positive and productive learning environment. In turn, the educator may find it increasingly difficult to create an inclusive classroom culture that encourages all students to engage fully and equally, especially when microaggressions undermine their authority and undermine the efforts to build relationships based on mutual respect.

> **Anecdote:** *I had Ms. Cunningham in the 6th grade. She was no joke. Everybody knew she didn't play, so it wasn't no use in even trying her. When she came around, people sat up straight, and other students stopped using inappropriate language because they knew she didn't like that. Ms. Cunningham had this presence that commanded respect, even before she said a word. Her no-nonsense attitude made you think twice before stepping out of line. It wasn't just her strictness; it was how she carried herself like she knew her worth and wasn't about to tolerate anyone questioning it. I remember how she could stop a whole room with just a look. When she walked into the teacher's lounge, teachers who would normally be cracking jokes or gossiping would quiet down immediately. It was like her authority went beyond just the classroom, kinda like it was a force that kept everything in check.*

Interactions With Parents and Administrators

Racial microaggressions also infiltrate the interactions that Black male educators have with parents and school administrators, adding yet another layer of complexity to their professional experiences. One of the most pervasive forms of microaggressions in these settings is the dismissal or devaluation of

Black male educators' perspectives and contributions, particularly in environments where leadership or parent bodies are predominantly white. This marginalization mirrors a larger societal tendency to undervalue the voices of Black individuals, especially when they hold positions of power or authority (Howard, 2013). In many cases, when suggestions or insights are offered by Black male educators, the response from colleagues or administrators is often muted or entirely dismissive. Despite years of experience and a deep understanding of students' needs, these educators' expertise is often sidelined, while the voices of others are amplified simply due to their racial background.

This dynamic can lead to frustration and disillusionment, as Black male educators may begin to feel as though their contributions are being ignored or undervalued. It becomes a constant reminder that, despite qualifications, experience, and dedication, these educators are expected to prove themselves more than their peers. What makes this even more frustrating is that in many cases, Black male educators are the ones best equipped to address the unique challenges faced by students from diverse backgrounds. Yet, their ideas are often marginalized, leaving them feeling like outsiders in a profession to which they have committed their careers. This undermines their sense of belonging within the very system they are working to improve.

Another form of microaggression frequently directed at Black male educators is the assumption that they are not *fitting* or *appropriate* for leadership roles, particularly in contexts where race plays an outsized role in perceptions of competence. The expectations that Black male educators face often center around a false narrative of what leadership should look like, traditionally, a demeanor that conforms to white, often gendered, expectations of authority. As a result, Black male educators are often overlooked for leadership positions or denied opportunities for professional growth, despite being highly qualified. This not only limits the professional advancement of Black male educators but also restricts the diversity and effectiveness of school leadership, ultimately affecting the students who benefit from a broad range of perspectives.

The effects of racial microaggressions in these interactions are compounded by racially biased evaluations and lower expectations placed on Black male educators by administrators. These biases are often informed by deeply ingrained stereotypes that question the leadership abilities of Black educators or assume they are less capable of handling complex teaching and administrative responsibilities (Williams, 1997). As a result, Black male educators may be passed over for leadership roles, denied opportunities for professional development, or unfairly judged during performance evaluations. This systemic bias can limit their career advancement and reinforce the notion that they are not fully equipped to thrive within the educational system. In contrast, white educators often do not face these same biased assumptions about their capabilities or leadership potential, further exacerbating the inequities that Black male educators experience in the workplace.

Anecdote: *There was a moment in my career that still stings when I think about it. I had been teaching for several years and had worked hard to build strong relationships with my students, parents, and colleagues. When a leadership position opened up at the school, I thought, This is my chance. I had the experience, the respect of my peers, and a deep understanding of what our students needed. I felt sure that I was the right person for the job. But when the principal made the announcement, I was shocked to hear that someone else had been chosen. I remember sitting there, trying to keep my face neutral, but inside I felt completely deflated. The person who was selected had less experience and a less personal connection to the students, yet somehow, they were the choice. I couldn't shake the feeling that my qualifications didn't matter as much as how I was perceived. It felt like my race and gender were standing in the way of my professional growth. As I watched someone else step into that role, I felt overlooked and undervalued, despite all the hard work I had put in. It was a painful reminder of how, as a Black male educator, even when you're qualified, you can still be passed over for opportunities simply because of who you are.*

The experience of being overlooked for a leadership role despite having the qualifications and strong relationships with students, parents, and colleagues is a stark reminder of the challenges that Black male educators often face in the professional world. It's not just about being passed over for a position; it's about the feeling that years of hard work and dedication are overshadowed by racial and gender biases. In many ways, this situation highlights the harsh reality that, for Black male educators, even those who are most deserving can be disregarded. However, these experiences also fuel a sense of resilience, a determination to rise above these challenges and not let them define one's worth or professional trajectory. Just as the Black Panther Party resisted systemic oppression, Black male educators must navigate a system that often minimizes their contributions and leadership potential. They must not only endure these obstacles but actively confront them, pushing back against forces that seek to limit their advancement. In doing so, they can create space for their voices to be heard and their leadership to be recognized in the educational landscape. To truly thrive, Black male educators need not only to survive but to empower themselves, equipping themselves with strategies to confront microaggressions and the systemic barriers they face.

Learning to Thrive

Black male educators, like their counterparts in the broader community, will inevitably encounter microaggressions and occasionally, more overt macroaggressions. Though these challenges may not be as frequent as the direct discrimination seen in other spheres, they are no less impactful. Much like the Black Panther Party's fierce resistance against police brutality and the systemic surveillance of Black communities, Black male educators must resist the forces that seek to undermine their presence, contributions, and advancement in the teaching profession. To truly thrive, Black male educators must not only endure but also actively confront the subtle and overt forces that seek to diminish them, cultivating a bank of strategies that will allow them to navigate these obstacles with resilience and experience more joy in their work.

The Black Panther Party boldly articulated a 10-point program to outline their vision for social justice and equality, and in much the same way, Black male educators can adopt their own 10-point program, a roadmap for resistance to microaggressions and an assertion of their worth and power in the classroom. Below, we detail such a program, designed to empower Black male educators and ensure their rightful place within the educational system. Below is a roadmap that offers guidance for this journey, inspired by the same principles of resistance and empowerment that shaped the Black Panther Party's fight for social justice.

Document Incidents of Microaggressions

It is essential to keep a thorough and detailed record of microaggressions that occur in your professional environment. By noting the date, time, individuals involved, and the nature of the incident, you create an invaluable log that can reveal patterns over time. This documentation can serve as evidence if you need to report the microaggressions to your administration or seek legal support. Not only does it ensure that your experiences are taken seriously, but it can also act as a tool for advocacy. Tracking these incidents helps illuminate the frequency and impact of the microaggressions, offering a more compelling argument when requesting institutional changes. In addition, a personal log provides an opportunity to reflect on how you've responded to these incidents, which can inform future strategies for handling microaggressions.

Example: A Black male educator might document an incident where a colleague remarks, "You're so articulate, for someone who looks like you." By logging the time, date, and details, the educator can highlight recurring moments of racial stereotyping to support their case when discussing the issue with the administration.

Develop and Practice Response Strategies

Anticipating and preparing for microaggressions equips you with the confidence to handle them when they arise. In a high-stress or emotionally charged environment, having practiced responses allows you to maintain your composure and act intentionally. Whether you choose a direct confrontation or a more passive response, practicing these strategies builds emotional resilience. Role-playing different scenarios with trusted colleagues or mentors can help refine your approach and reduce feelings of being caught off guard. In addition, practicing self-reflection and mindfulness techniques can ensure your responses align with your values and prevent unnecessary escalation. It's crucial to develop responses that educate others about the impact of their behavior while maintaining professional integrity. *Example:* A Black male educator might practice a response to a colleague who comments on his *intimidating* presence in the classroom. By calmly explaining how such a comment reinforces harmful stereotypes and discussing the negative impact it has, the educator can address the microaggression without becoming defensive.

Seek Leadership Roles and Advocate for Change

Taking on leadership roles within your school or district provides you with the platform to influence policies and practices surrounding diversity, equity, and inclusion. Black male educators who occupy leadership positions can initiate meaningful changes that challenge the microaggressions embedded within the culture. These roles also allow you to model inclusive leadership for students and staff, showing that systemic change is possible. Being in a leadership position provides a broader lens through which to advocate for the integration of antibias programs, more equitable teacher evaluations, and the creation of safer, more inclusive spaces for all educators and students. While leadership roles can be challenging, they allow you to actively shape the institutional environment and amplify marginalized voices. *Example:* A Black male educator might apply for a leadership role in the diversity and inclusion committee, where he can influence the curriculum to include more culturally responsive teaching methods and organize training on microaggressions for staff.

Advocate for Racial and Cultural Awareness Programs

Instituting racial and cultural awareness programs is a crucial way to address microaggressions before they escalate. These programs can help dismantle stereotypes and prejudices, promoting empathy and understanding among students and staff. By educating others on the historical and social roots of microaggressions and racial bias, you are creating an environment where such behavior is less likely to be tolerated. Furthermore, awareness programs can foster a proactive approach to addressing microaggressions, encouraging colleagues and students to recognize their biases and take responsibility for their actions. Advocacy for such programs should focus on sustained dialogue and tangible actions, not just one-time workshops or lectures, to ensure meaningful impact. *Example:* A Black male educator might push for a school-wide initiative where students and teachers participate in a series of workshops discussing the origins of racial stereotypes, microaggressions, and their effects on individuals, especially in educational environments.

Create Space for Open Conversations About Race and Gender

Opening the door for candid discussions about race, gender, and microaggressions fosters a culture of inclusivity and reflection. By facilitating conversations on these topics, you allow space for individuals to examine their own biases and how these biases may manifest in subtle actions. These discussions can promote a deeper understanding of privilege and power dynamics in education and lead to greater empathy between educators and students. Creating a safe, nonjudgmental environment for these conversations means everyone feels empowered to contribute, share experiences, and work toward collective solutions. Additionally, these dialogues can help shift school culture from one of silence and denial to one of openness and accountability. *Example:* A Black male educator might initiate a weekly discussion group among teachers about their experiences with race in the classroom, allowing colleagues to share their own encounters with bias, reflect on their behavior, and commit to making changes.

Invest in Professional Counseling or Therapy

The emotional and psychological toll of constant microaggressions cannot be underestimated, and seeking professional counseling or therapy is an essential self-care practice. Therapy, especially with professionals who specialize in race-related stress, can help Black male educators process the anger, frustration, and emotional fatigue that arise from daily exposure to microaggressions. These specialists can also help develop coping mechanisms, such as stress management techniques, cognitive reframing, and boundary-setting, that allow educators to manage their emotional well-being effectively. Mental health professionals can provide valuable support, not only in addressing the emotional aftermath of microaggressions but also in building resilience and emotional intelligence to handle future incidents. Seeking therapy ensures that educators don't internalize the pain from microaggressions, preserving their long-term mental and emotional health. *Example:* A Black male educator may seek therapy after experiencing a series of undermining comments from colleagues, learning tools to manage stress, and developing strategies to maintain emotional balance in the face of ongoing microaggressions.

Recognize Your Value and Expertise

Black male educators must consistently remind themselves of their value and professional worth. Microaggressions often serve to undermine confidence, and if left unchecked, they can lead to a weakened sense of professional identity. Engaging in positive self-affirmation practices, such as reflecting on past successes, positive feedback from students, and contributions to the school community, can counteract the negative effects of microaggressions. By grounding themselves in their expertise and accomplishments, Black male educators can resist internalizing the harmful stereotypes imposed by others. Regularly reinforcing one's self-worth fosters a sense of pride in the profession and provides the emotional fortitude needed to confront microaggressions with grace and strength. *Example:* A Black male educator might take time to reflect on his successful mentorship of students who have gone on to excel academically, using these affirmations to counter the discouraging effects of microaggressions that question his authority.

Set Clear Expectations for Respect

Establishing and communicating clear boundaries for respect in the classroom or professional setting can help mitigate microaggressions. Proactively addressing what constitutes respectful behavior with students, colleagues, and administrators establishes a standard for conduct that fosters mutual respect. This preemptive strategy can help reduce instances of microaggressions by making it clear from the outset that such behavior will not be tolerated. It also sets a precedent for how you expect to be treated, offering guidance for those who may not be aware of their own biases or inappropriate actions. Consistent reinforcement of these boundaries helps create a professional atmosphere that is conducive to inclusivity and mutual respect, making it less likely for microaggressions to occur. *Example:* A Black male educator might begin every class by setting clear expectations about how students should address him and others, stressing the importance of respect and inclusivity and explaining that any disrespectful comments will be addressed immediately.

Engage in Restorative Practices

Restorative practices, when used effectively, can help repair relationships after microaggressions and create an opportunity for deeper understanding. Instead of relying solely on punitive measures, restorative practices emphasize dialogue, mutual accountability, and emotional healing. These practices allow Black male educators to express how the microaggressions affected them and create a space for others to reflect on their actions. Engaging in restorative practices can also promote empathy and foster positive behavioral changes among students and colleagues. Moreover, restorative circles and discussions can be used proactively, creating a culture where issues related to race, respect, and microaggressions are addressed before they escalate. *Example:* After a microaggression from a student, a Black male educator might arrange a restorative circle where the student can explain their perspective, the educator shares how it made them feel, and they work together to repair the relationship through open communication.

Advocate for Institutional Change

Advocacy for institutional policies that specifically address microaggressions is essential in building a school culture that prioritizes diversity, equity, and inclusion. As a Black male educator, advocating for policy changes such as the inclusion of microaggressions in antibias training, the creation of diversity-focused recruitment initiatives, and the integration of multicultural perspectives in curriculum development can be powerful strategies for institutional reform. By working toward professional development opportunities that educate staff on microaggressions and implicit bias, educators can help shift school culture toward one that recognizes the impact of racial discrimination and takes active steps to remedy it. Additionally, advocating for policies that hold individuals accountable for microaggressions and ensuring there are systems in place for reporting and addressing these issues can help create a more supportive and respectful environment for both educators and students. *Example:* A Black male educator might work with the school's equity committee to push for the implementation of mandatory anti-racism training for all staff and advocate for clearer protocols to report and address microaggressions in the school setting.

Conclusion

The challenges faced by Black male educators are multifaceted, shaped not only by overt forms of racial discrimination but also by the insidious impact of microaggressions. These subtle yet persistent acts of racial bias, often dismissed by those who do not share the same experiences, contribute to a cumulative emotional and psychological strain that influences both professional identities and personal well-being. This ongoing battle for recognition, dignity, and respect is navigated daily by many Black male educators, often without the necessary support or understanding from colleagues or institutions.

The legacy of the Black Panther Party for Self-Defense has profoundly influenced approaches to work in the classroom. The Party's core principles of resistance, empowerment, and community advocacy were not solely about protesting injustice; they were about creating tangible, life-changing programs that directly addressed systemic issues. For Black male educators, the role extends far beyond imparting academic knowledge. Similar to the Black Panther Party's community programs, such as the Free Breakfast for Children and Liberation Schools, the mission is to uplift and empower students, particularly those who are often marginalized by society. Educators within this context are part of a broader movement, dedicated not only to teaching but to creating spaces where students can recognize their value, resilience, and potential in the face of systemic adversity.

This understanding deepens the connection between the fight for educational equity and the fight for racial justice. The same systems that oppress communities outside the classroom also shape educational environments within them. Just as the Black Panther Party sought to dismantle systems of inequality, educators must continue to challenge and confront the racial biases that permeate schools. The work is not just about educating minds; it is about transforming lives, building a sense of dignity, pride, and empowerment in students. The Black Panther Party's legacy serves as both a guiding light and a call to action, reminding all that the struggle for justice is ongoing. Black male educators bear the responsibility of standing firm in this fight, ensuring that the next generation of students not only survives but thrives in a world that often seeks to hold them back.

To Thrive, Black male educators should

1. Document Incidents of Microaggressions
2. Develop and Practice Response Strategies
3. Seek Leadership Roles and Advocate for Change
4. Advocate for Racial and Cultural Awareness Programs
5. Create Space for Open Conversations About Race and Gender
6. Invest in Professional Counseling or Therapy
7. Recognize Your Value and Expertise
8. Set Clear Expectations for Respect
9. Engage in Restorative Practices
10. Advocate for Institutional Change

Questions for Reflection

1. In what ways can the Black Panther Party's community-focused programs, like the Free Breakfast for Children, inspire educational practices that benefit marginalized students today?
2. How can schools and districts integrate training programs that address microaggressions and promote racial equity in professional development for educators?
3. What are the potential benefits and challenges of creating safe spaces for Black male educators to discuss their experiences with microaggressions and systemic racism in schools?

References

Berry, T. R. (2018). Racial microaggressions in education: A transformative framework for teaching and learning. *The Review of Black Political Economy, 45*(4), 471–494.

Clark, R., Anderson, N. B., Clark, V. R., & Williams, D. R. (1999). Racism as a stressor in the mental health of African Americans: A biopsychosocial model. *American Psychologist, 54*(10), 805–816.

Howard, T. C. (2013). How does it feel to be a problem? Black male students, schools, and learning in enhancing the knowledge base to disrupt deficit frameworks. *Review of Research in Education, 37*(1), 54–86.

Smith, W. A., Allen, W. R., & Danley, L. L. (2007). "Assume the position...": Understanding the working experiences of Black faculty members. *Journal of Negro Education, 76*(3), 348–364.

Solórzano, D. G., Ceja, M., & Yosso, T. J. (2000). Critical race theory, racial microaggressions, and the experience of Chicana and Chicano students. *International Journal of Qualitative Studies in Education, 13*(4), 423–451.

Sue, D. W., Capodilupo, C. M., Torino, G. C., Bucceri, J. M., Holder, A. M. B., Nadal, K. L., & Esquilin, M. (2007). Racial microaggressions in everyday life: Implications for clinical practice. *American Psychologist, 62*(4), 271–286.

Williams, D. R. (1997). Racism and health: A research agenda for the 21st century. *The International Journal of Health Services, 27*(3), 257–266.

CHAPTER 7

THRIVING WITH RADICAL CLASSROOM INSTRUCTION: APPLYING BLACK PANTHER PARTY IDEALS TO FOSTER CRITICAL THINKING

In the previous chapter, I referenced the history of the Black Panther Party (BPP) and identified Huey P. Newton and Bobby Seale as the founders of this impactful organization. Despite all the attention to their armed resistance to oppression, the Panthers also provided instructive guidance on the need to educate the children in underserved communities, and Black male educators can learn a great deal from their actions. The Black Panther Party's educational initiatives, such as the Free Breakfast for Children Program and the Oakland Community School (OCS), were instrumental in fostering critical thinking and resilience in the face of systemic oppression. These programs not only met the immediate needs of the community but also served as a form of resistance by empowering the youth with knowledge and instilling in them a sense of pride and purpose. By incorporating these values into modern teaching practices, Black male educators can adopt a similar approach, viewing education as a tool for social transformation rather than merely a way to impart academic knowledge.

Through mentorship, community engagement, and activism, Black male educators have the potential to create classroom environments that reflect the Panthers' vision of social justice, equity, and self-determination, inspiring children and future generations to think critically and empower themselves.

The OCS, founded in 1973 by the BPP in Oakland, California, was not just an educational institution; it was a revolutionary act in itself. At a time when the educational system largely ignored the needs of Black children in marginalized communities, the OCS sought to create an alternative that was rooted in justice, empowerment, and collective progress (Seale, 1991). The BPP, understanding that traditional schools often served as vehicles of oppression rather than liberation, established the OCS as a space where Black children could develop not only academically but also socially, emotionally, and politically (Davis, 1981). The curriculum was intentionally designed to foster critical thinking, self-determination, and a deep understanding of social justice, with a strong emphasis on Black history and culture (Ture & Hamilton, 1967). This was an education that challenged students to question authority, critically examine societal structures, and use their knowledge as a weapon for social change (Newton, 1973). In many ways, the OCS aimed to equip young people with the tools to rewrite their own narratives, ones that had long been written for them by systems of oppression.

What set the OCS apart was its holistic approach to education. The BPP recognized that for children to succeed academically, they first needed their basic needs met, and they needed to feel nurtured and supported. The school provided not only free breakfast and healthcare but also after-school programs designed to ensure that every child had the opportunity to thrive, physically, mentally, and emotionally. This integrated model reinforced the belief that education cannot be separated from the lived realities of the community. Teachers at OCS were not merely instructors; they were activists and community leaders, working hand in hand with parents to instill values of pride, resilience, and collective responsibility. They taught their students to value their cultural heritage, to embrace their identity, and to see themselves as agents of change capable of confronting the systemic injustices in their lives (Jeffries, 2019). The school wasn't just about preparing children for the world; it was about preparing them to change it.

Educational Challenges

Within educational schemes, schools are struggling to support students to achieve positive academic outcomes on standardized tests. According to the National Assessment of Educational Progress (NAEP), achievement gaps persist across racial and socioeconomic groups, with Black and Hispanic students often scoring lower than their White counterparts in subjects such as mathematics and reading. These gaps highlight not just disparities in test scores but the deeper, systemic inequalities that influence educational outcomes. These disparities are indicative of an education system that historically has underfunded and underserved minority communities, thus exacerbating the challenges faced by Black and Hispanic students. As Darling-Hammond (2010) argues, students from underprivileged backgrounds frequently lack access to high-quality instructional materials and experienced teachers, two critical components that contribute to higher performance on standardized tests.

Moreover, the pressures of standardized testing often overlook the unique cultural, emotional, and social contexts of students from marginalized communities. These tests are inherently designed in ways that may not always resonate with students' lived experiences, often leading to disengagement and reduced motivation (Ladson-Billings, 2006). This phenomenon is exacerbated by implicit bias in educational settings, where teachers' expectations can be influenced by stereotypes, inadvertently leading to lower performance expectations for minority students. These issues are compounded by school policies that prioritize test preparation over more holistic, culturally relevant educational practices that support student identity and personal growth. As Kozol (2012) notes, schools in low-income neighborhoods often lack the resources to provide students with the comprehensive educational experiences they need to succeed beyond test scores.

The Free Breakfast for Children Program

One of the most well-known programs initiated by the BPP was the Free Breakfast for Children Program, launched in 1969. This program sought to address hunger in Black communities, recognizing that children could not perform well academically without proper nutrition. By providing free breakfasts to children in underserved communities, the Panthers demonstrated that basic needs must be met before academic learning can take place. This initiative was not just about feeding children but also about challenging the neglect and disinvestment in Black neighborhoods. The Free Breakfast Program served thousands of children daily in major cities like Oakland, Los Angeles, and Chicago, exemplifying the Party's understanding of the interconnection between education, social services, and activism. The program was revolutionary because it addressed the immediate physical needs of children while fostering a deeper understanding of the systemic issues at play. It empowered parents and students by showing them that the community could organize and take care of its own, bypassing the neglect of state institutions. Black male educators can learn from this program by recognizing that holistic education includes not only academics but also the emotional, physical, and social needs of their students.

Moreover, the Free Breakfast Program instilled a profound sense of pride and solidarity within the community. It not only addressed a critical need but also fostered a sense of dignity for children who, in many cases, may have otherwise felt invisible or unworthy in a society that often overlooked their struggles. For these children, this program became more than just a meal; it was a reminder that they mattered, that their needs were important, and that they deserved care and attention. For Black male educators, this initiative represents a vital teaching philosophy, one centered around creating a nurturing, inclusive environment where students feel seen and valued. It emphasizes the importance of recognizing the whole child, honoring their worth, and providing the emotional support necessary for them to thrive, not just academically, but personally. This approach transcends the classroom, impacting students' lives beyond school walls, showing them that they have a place in the world and that their voices and experiences are worth acknowledging.

The Oakland Community School (OCS)

The OCS, founded in 1973 by the BPP, remains one of the most enduring legacies of the Panthers' commitment to education and the empowerment of Black communities. At the time of its inception, public schools in Black neighborhoods were often overcrowded, underfunded, and dismissive of the cultural and educational needs of Black children. Many of these institutions provided subpar education that failed to engage with the complexities of Black history or the realities of systemic oppression. OCS sought to offer a radically different approach—one that was rooted in academic excellence and social justice while celebrating the cultural richness of Black identity. The founders understood that education could be both a tool for personal success and a means for collective liberation.

The curriculum at OCS was designed not only to meet high academic standards but also to encourage critical thinking, self-determination, and political awareness. Students were empowered to challenge societal structures, question the status quo, and examine their roles in the world through the lens of justice and activism. Education at OCS was never passive; it was an active, dynamic tool for shaping the future. Teachers were encouraged to guide students toward understanding how their learning could contribute to meaningful social change. This was a school that believed in teaching students to be change-makers, to view the world critically, and to use their education to disrupt systems that sought to marginalize them.

The educators at OCS were not merely teachers in the traditional sense. They were activists, mentors, and community leaders, deeply invested in their students' futures and the broader struggle for Black liberation. They saw themselves as part of a larger movement, connecting the classroom to the streets, the home, and the broader community. Teachers worked hand-in-hand with parents to create a holistic educational experience that went beyond academic instruction. This partnership reinforced the idea that the work of education was not just the responsibility of the school but of the entire community. Together, they strived to build a safe and nurturing environment where children could not only succeed academically but also feel proud of their cultural heritage and empowered to act with a sense of purpose.

At OCS, the emphasis was not solely on academic success but also on instilling values of unity, collective responsibility, and community service. These values helped students see themselves as part of a larger movement for social justice, reminding them that their actions had the potential to create lasting change. This sense of collective responsibility was integral to the school's mission, teaching students that true progress comes when individuals work together to support and uplift each other. OCS thus became a place where students learned that education is not just about acquiring knowledge but about using that knowledge to make a difference in the world.

In addition to academic subjects, the school placed a strong emphasis on Black history and culture, encouraging students to take pride in their identity and to learn about the struggles and triumphs of their ancestors. This focus on cultural education was crucial in helping students feel a sense of belonging, grounded in a rich legacy of resistance, resilience, and empowerment. By understanding their place in history, students could better understand the significance of their own potential and the impact they could have on the world. The school's curriculum also prioritized political education, teaching students about their rights and the importance of civic engagement. They learned how to organize for social change, how to challenge injustice, and how to use their voices to advocate for a more equitable society.

OCS represented a revolutionary model of education, one that transcended traditional schooling to address the broader needs of the community. It was a space where education and activism were intertwined, with students being taught not just to excel academically but also to understand their role in fighting for justice. The school's holistic approach emphasized that education should not be limited to preparing students for jobs; it should prepare them to be leaders in the fight for social change. The legacy of OCS continues to serve as a reminder that education must address not only intellectual development but also social consciousness and collective action.

Anecdote: *I grew up in Oakland, and I remember hearing about the Black Panther schools. I always wanted to go, but my parents were a bit hesitant. Those schools were different from anything I had ever seen—there was this energy about them, this sense that education was about more than just reading and writing. It was about learning how to live with purpose, to question things, and to understand your place in the world. I'd see Panthers around town, at rallies or in the streets, always pushing for change and making sure Black people's voices were heard. As a kid, I didn't fully get what they were about, but I could tell it was something important.*

My parents, though they supported the Panthers' work in the community, were wary of their strong beliefs and the whole "militant" vibe. They just wanted me to have a good future, so they figured public school was the safer option. But even then, I couldn't shake this feeling that there was something special about those Black Panther schools. They weren't just schools; they were about resistance, about saying, "We deserve more than what the system is giving us." The Panthers believed Black kids should have an education that didn't just teach us facts, but taught us how to think for ourselves, understand what was happening in our communities, and fight for change.

I never got to attend one of those schools, but the lessons they were pushing still stick with me. The idea that education is about more than just memorizing facts, that it's about empowerment, understanding who you are, and what you can do to change things, has shaped how I think about learning today. Even though I didn't walk those halls, I carry that legacy with me, and it influences the way I want to help young people now. I want them to feel seen, heard, and strong enough to challenge the world around them, just like the Panthers taught.

The Connection Between Black Male Educators and the BPP

The educational philosophy of the BPP provides a powerful and relevant framework for Black male educators today, as it emphasizes the necessity of education as a tool for empowerment, liberation, and social change. The BPP recognized that education was not just about academic achievement but about cultivating a broader political awareness, social consciousness, and self-determination within students, particularly within marginalized communities. According to the BPP, true education must address the whole child, mind, body, and spirit, by fostering an understanding of self, community, and the broader socio-political structures that shape their lives (Newton, 1973). For Black male educators, this philosophy offers invaluable lessons on how to go beyond the confines of traditional schooling and nurture students who are capable of critical thinking, activism, and leadership.

The BPP's educational initiatives were grounded in the belief that knowledge is power and that oppressed communities must control their own education to break free from systemic injustice and inequality (Seale, 1991). Programs such as the OCS and the Free Breakfast for Children Program were not only aimed at addressing immediate community needs but also worked to dismantle the oppressive structures in place by empowering young people through education. The BPP viewed education as an essential means of promoting resistance to the status quo, offering an opportunity for marginalized communities to gain control over their own narratives and destinies. Black male educators, inspired by these initiatives, must understand that true education is not merely the transmission of knowledge but the cultivation of critical consciousness, where students learn not just to absorb information but to actively question and challenge the world around them.

For Black male educators today, this philosophy means creating spaces where students can engage with the world beyond textbooks, develop critical awareness of societal structures, and see themselves as agents of change. The goal is not just to teach content but to help students think critically about their roles in society and their capacity to challenge injustices they encounter. Drawing from the BPP's principles, educators should encourage students to view their education as a tool for resistance, empowering them to understand the complexities of history, politics, and economics, and how these intersect with race, class, and identity (Rodriguez, 2013). The Panthers saw education as a means of personal and collective liberation, asserting that knowledge should not only inform but also transform (Bing, 2006). Thus, Black male educators can empower students by making education not a passive experience but an active process of interrogation and resistance.

The BPP's educational model challenges educators to move beyond conventional pedagogies that focus solely on academic achievement. Instead, it suggests that education should nurture a sense of agency in students, inspiring them to question the social, political, and economic systems that shape their lives. As Black male educators, embracing the BPP's philosophy means creating classrooms that promote critical engagement with the world, where students are encouraged to ask difficult questions, challenge authority, and develop the skills necessary to create meaningful social change. This approach to education remains particularly significant in today's educational landscape, where students, especially those from marginalized communities, often encounter systems of oppression and inequality that seek to limit their potential. By adopting the BPP's vision, Black male educators can provide a powerful counter-narrative, helping students see themselves as active participants in shaping their futures, rather than passive recipients of knowledge.

The educational philosophy of the BPP offers an essential blueprint for Black male educators who seek to create environments where students can thrive academically, socially, and politically. By embracing the BPP's emphasis on critical thinking, political awareness, and self-determination, educators can help students develop the tools they need to navigate and challenge the societal systems that affect their lives. The Panthers understood that education is not a neutral or passive experience; it is a powerful tool for liberation and social change. Black male educators who embody this philosophy can foster classrooms that inspire students to become critical thinkers, activists, and leaders, ultimately contributing to the ongoing struggle for justice and equity in society.

> **Anecdote:** *The Black Panthers were some smart folks. I used to listen to Huey, Bobby, and Elaine Brown talk about politics, and I loved the way they reasoned. People who interviewed them could not keep up with the way they thought. My dad used to call them heavy, as in those are some <u>heavy</u> cats!*

For Black male educators, *thriving* is also a matter of their own empowerment. Drawing inspiration from the BPPs leaders, who were not only educators but activists and community leaders, Black male educators today can thrive by adopting the same philosophy of resistance, activism, and community leadership. Embracing this legacy means becoming more than just teachers; they can become mentors, role models, and advocates for their students, engaging in the ongoing struggle for racial justice and equity in education. Just as the Free Breakfast for Children Program empowered communities by addressing immediate needs and fostering a sense of solidarity, Black male educators can create environments where students not only succeed academically but also feel valued, heard, and supported. When Black male educators thrive, they create spaces where their students feel safe, seen, and empowered, paving the way for their success in the classroom and beyond, while simultaneously contributing to a greater community movement for justice and equality.

Learning to Thrive

The BPPs emphasis on self-determination and activism offers Black male educators a powerful framework for their own empowerment. The Panthers emphasized the importance of questioning authority, whether it be teachers, government leaders, or societal norms. This was especially important in the context of an educational system that often marginalized Black students, treating them as inferior or less capable. By encouraging students to question authority, Black male educators can help dismantle this mentality and empower them to seek truth and justice. Moreover, when students thrive, Black male educators thrive as well. Thriving is not only about students' academic success but also about fostering a space where educators themselves can grow, feel valued, and connect with their purpose. Black male educators, by empowering their students to challenge oppressive systems, can also learn and evolve through the process. As they nurture critical thinking, self-awareness, and resilience in their students, they too gain insights into their own experiences and identities, ultimately thriving in their roles as mentors, leaders, and community advocates. The following techniques are examples of how Black male educators can empower their students to thrive academically, socially, and emotionally, while simultaneously cultivating their own growth and self-knowledge.

Holistic Education: Addressing the Whole Child

The BPP understood that true education wasn't just about academic success, but about nurturing the whole child, socially, emotionally, and politically. Black male educators can thrive by adopting a holistic approach to teaching, where they care for their students' emotional well-being and personal growth just as much as their academic achievements. This approach reflects the BPP's commitment to meeting the needs of the whole community, not just providing academic content. For example, Black male educators can integrate social-emotional learning (SEL) into their curriculum. This could involve fostering a classroom culture where students feel comfortable discussing their challenges, affirming their cultural identities, and receiving the emotional and psychological support they need to navigate their lives outside of school. Educators can also build mentorship programs to help students deal with trauma, microaggressions, and systemic discrimination, similar to how the BPP provided community services to address immediate needs.

Critical Thinking and Political Education

The BPP's educational philosophy emphasized critical thinking and political consciousness. Black male educators can thrive by teaching students to engage critically with the world around them and empowering them to question the status quo. By fostering a deep sense of political awareness and historical understanding, educators can empower students to not only excel in school but also to actively engage with their communities and challenge injustice. For instance, educators can incorporate discussions about systemic racism, historical oppression, and social justice into their curriculum. Teaching students their history not merely as a subject, but as a tool for empowerment, allows students to understand their heritage and the ongoing struggle for justice. Encouraging students to think critically about current events and the power structures in society equips them to be active participants in creating social change, aligning with the BPP's belief that education should help people understand and resist systems of oppression.

Community-Centered Education

The BPP was deeply committed to the community, recognizing that education is a collective effort. Black male educators can thrive by creating strong connections between their classrooms and the broader community, drawing on the Panthers' model of activism and mutual aid. In doing so, educators not only teach their students but also foster a sense of responsibility toward community well-being. For example, Black male educators can organize community events, involve parents in the educational process, and partner with local organizations to provide resources for students. Hosting after-school programs, tutoring sessions, or neighborhood clean-up initiatives can engage students and families in collective community-building efforts. Just as the BPP's Free Breakfast for Children Program and health clinics were community-driven initiatives, Black male educators can help their students understand the value of solidarity, mutual aid, and collective action in the face of systemic challenges.

Building Cultural Pride and Identity

The BPP placed a strong emphasis on Black cultural pride, encouraging Black children to see themselves as part of a rich legacy of resistance, resilience, and achievement. Black male educators can thrive by instilling pride in their students' cultural identities and helping them connect with their heritage, fostering a sense of empowerment and belonging. For example, Black male educators can create culturally relevant curricula that celebrate Black history, art, music, and literature. This could involve teaching Black authors, poets, and historians, for example, or celebrating Black cultural contributions through music, dance, and art. Educators can also create projects that allow students to explore their own family histories and cultural backgrounds, helping them see themselves as part of a larger, vibrant tradition that spans generations of resistance and achievement.

Empowerment Through Activism and Leadership

The BPP encouraged activism and self-determination, believing that true education empowered individuals to take action and create social change. Black male educators can thrive by positioning themselves not only as instructors but also as leaders, mentors, and activists who inspire students to take action in their communities and beyond. By empowering students to become agents of change, educators help them understand their own potential to affect the world. For example, educators can cultivate leadership skills in students by involving them in social justice projects, leadership roles in the classroom, or activism initiatives. Organizing a student group that focuses on racial justice or community improvement can encourage students to take ownership of their education and their role in society. By modeling activism, Black male educators can demonstrate the power of collective action and encourage students to use their voices for social good.

Fostering a Safe and Inclusive Learning Environment

The BPP's approach to education focused on creating a safe and inclusive space for learning, where students could thrive without the fear of discrimination or marginalization. Black male educators can thrive by creating classrooms where all students feel valued, respected, and supported, regardless of their background or identity. This environment of respect and inclusivity encourages students to fully engage in their education. For example, Black male educators can work to ensure that their classrooms are safe spaces where students can freely express themselves. They can establish clear anti-racism policies, foster open dialogue about discrimination, and incorporate inclusive teaching practices that respect students' identities and lived experiences. Educators can focus on building a strong classroom community where each student's voice is heard, mirroring the BPP's emphasis on unity and solidarity within Black communities.

Mentorship and Role Modeling

The BPP believed that educators should be more than just teachers—they should be role models, mentors, and leaders within their communities. Black male educators can thrive by embracing these roles and providing mentorship to their students, particularly those who may lack positive male role models in their lives. By providing guidance and support, educators can have a lasting impact on the personal and academic development of their students. For example, Black male educators can offer one-on-one mentorship to students, helping them navigate both academic and personal challenges. Sharing their own experiences, struggles, and successes can show students that they, too, can overcome obstacles and achieve their goals. This mentorship extends beyond the classroom, building relationships that help students thrive both inside and outside of school. By being a positive presence in students' lives, educators can offer the kind of guidance that shapes their futures and nurtures their growth.

Conclusion

The BPPs legacy continues to offer invaluable lessons for Black male educators today. Their revolutionary approach to education, one that fused academic learning with political consciousness, community engagement, and social activism, serves as a model for how education can be a tool for social change. Black male educators, by drawing on the lessons of the Panthers, can create classrooms that not only foster academic excellence but also cultivate the critical thinking, self-determination, and social justice values necessary for students to challenge the systems of oppression they encounter. The work of the Panthers is far from over, and the challenge of continuing their fight for justice and equity in education remains as urgent today as it was in the 1960s and 1970s. Black male educators, empowered by this vision, can continue the fight for an education system that truly serves all students, especially those from marginalized communities, by transforming education from a mechanism of oppression into one of liberation.

To Thrive, Black male educators should:

1. Provide Holistic Education and Addressing the Whole Child
2. Teach Critical Thinking and Political Education
3. Provide Community-Centered Education
4. Build Cultural Pride and Identity
5. Be able to Build Empowerment Through Activism and Leadership
6. Have Chances to Foster a Safe and Inclusive Learning Environment
7. Have Mentorship and Role Modeling Opportunities

Questions for Reflection

1. What does it mean to nurture a community-centered approach to education, and how can Black male educators build stronger connections between the classroom, students' families, and the broader community to support student success?
2. How can Black male educators create a classroom environment that challenges the status quo, fosters critical thinking, and encourages students to question authority, while also providing a safe, inclusive space where all students feel seen and valued?
3. In what ways can Black male educators empower their students to not only succeed academically but also to engage critically with social issues, challenge systemic injustice, and participate in activism, as inspired by the BPPs educational philosophy?

References

Bing, L. (2006). Knowledge as liberation: The educational philosophy of the Black Panther party. *Journal of Education, 39*(2), 104-120.
Darling-Hammond, L. (2010). *The flat world and education: How America's commitment to equity will determine our future.* Teachers College Press.
Davis, A. (1981). *Women, race, and class.* Random House.
Jeffries, M. (2019). Critical education and Black empowerment: Lessons from the Black Panther party. *Journal of Educational Change, 12*(4), 234–250.
Kozol, J. (2012). *Savage inequalities: Children in America's schools.* Harper Collins.

Ladson-Billings, G. (2006). From the achievement gap to the education debt: Understanding achievement in U.S. schools. *Educational Researcher, 35*(7), 3–12.

Newton, H. P. (1973). *Revolutionary suicide.* Harcourt Brace Jovanovich.

Rodriguez, N. (2013). The Black Panther party and its educational model: Teaching for liberation. *Journal of African American Studies, 17*(4), 45–62.

Seale, B. (1991). *Seize the time: The story of the Black Panther party and Huey P. Newton.* Black Classic Press.

Ture, K., & Hamilton, C. V. (1967). *Black power: The politics of liberation in America.* Random House.

AFTERWORD

There are approximately 50,000 Black male educators currently serving in public school spaces. While this number may seem significant at first glance, it's important to keep it in perspective. In the broader context, there are over 3 million public school teachers in the United States, and the overwhelming majority of them are white women. This creates a stark imbalance, one that deeply affects the classroom experience for many Black male educators. For myself, and I'm sure many others, the lack of Black male representation in teaching is not just a statistic; it's a lived reality. It's a presence that is missing, and its absence is often palpable. It can be alienating for those of us who, like me, entered education with a deep desire for affirmation, but instead found ourselves battling against the weight of impostor syndrome. The feeling of being one of the few, or sometimes the only, Black male in the room is isolating. It's not just about numbers, it's about the emotional and professional support that seems to be so scarce. And I'm sure I'm not alone in feeling this way. There are likely countless others who have experienced similar struggles, navigating a space where they are constantly reminded of how rare their presence is.

I want to take a moment to express my eternal gratitude to all the Black male educators who took the time to complete my survey. I know that filling out a survey is not exactly an exciting or glamorous task, but these gentlemen generously gave their time and shared their invaluable experiences. They provided me with a wealth of information about their personal journeys, their unique teaching contexts, and their thoughts on how to better support Black male teachers in this field. The insights I received were not only thoughtful, but they were a testament to the resilience, wisdom, and dedication of Black male educators who are working tirelessly, often without the recognition they deserve. To those men, thank you. Your contributions have not only enriched this project but have reaffirmed the importance of our voices and experiences in the conversation about education.

Black male teacherdom is not at all easy. It's a profession that demands resilience in the face of underrepresentation, misunderstanding, and often a lack of institutional support. We are often tasked with doing the emotional labor of being role models, mentors, and educators, all while trying to navigate a system that may not always recognize or appreciate the unique challenges we face. The weight of being an example for others, while also trying to carve out space for ourselves within an overwhelmingly white and female-dominated profession, is something that many Black male teachers carry with quiet strength. This work is often invisible, yet its impact is profound. It is a labor of love and a commitment to the next generation.

Lastly, I want to shout out some people who have been seminal in my journey to this point and for whom I have great respect. Shout out to Aunt Lois (Dr. Lois Webster Winston), Uncle Bill Winston, Dr. Gregory Lomack, Dr. Ernest Black, Dr. Kirk Kirkwood, Mr. Kempton Coman, Dr. Mahmoud Suleiman, Dr. Ken Magdaleno, Mr. Searcy Barnett, Carrie "C-Note" Sandles, my brilliant children, David, Drake, Daschl, and Daymon, Dr. Kristina LaGue, Mrs. Brenda Wells-Sandles, Mr. David Sandles, Sr., Ms. Shirley Sandles, Mr. Michael Davis, Ms. Georgia Ruth Davenport, Mr. Ray Uribe, Mr. Wayne Burris, and Kool Moe Dee. Some folks may see the name Kool Moe Dee and chuckle, but that man's music saved my life.

In gratitude,
David Sandles